Millions of *Woma*
Tessa Wood. Now
most intimate
meaningful ins
institution

Married Secrets

Tales from Tessa Wood

Futura

Illustrated by Penny Simon

A Futura Book

First published in Great Britain in 1984
by Futura Publications, a Division of
Macdonald & Co (Publishers) Ltd
London & Sydney

ISBN 0 7088 2615 6

Typeset, printed and bound in Great Britain by
Hazell Watson & Viney Limited
Member of the BPCC Group
Aylesbury, Bucks

Futura Publications
A Division of
Macdonald & Co (Publishers) Ltd
Maxwell House
74 Worship Street
London EC2A 2EN
A BPCC plc Company

Contents

CHAPTER ONE

Tears Before Bed

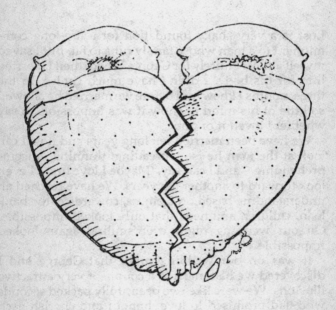

Lust is a very shaky foundation for a life-long commitment to a man whose family runs to fat. But I saved myself almost entirely for George Wood, then I married him for his body. I didn't have much choice. In the three months I knew him before we married he allowed so little of his mind to show it was impossible to say whether I loved it or not.

We have been married ten long years and now I can look at the man he is – spreading, thinning, uncomprehending – and I can say, 'Maybe I love him.' I even look forward to another ten years. We have reached an understanding based on laziness, cowardice, the bank loan, children and need that once looked impossible. On our wedding night ever smiling again looked impossible.

It was on our wedding night that George and I discovered we had married a couple of very attractive illusions. We were like two beautifully packed seconds who had promised to love, honour and cherish each other's wrapping. Our marriage has been a mystifying game of pass-the-parcel. What has mystified me is that it has lasted so long.

It began on a twin bed in a small hotel behind Victoria coach station, where I lay on the brink of divorce with nothing to reassure me apart from the low, gentle hum of the traffic and someone's sinus. 'Dear God,' I prayed, 'if there is a God. Tell me why I married. Tell me who I married. Tell me if the weather in Spain will make the honeymoon worth it.'

Married is a very lonely thing to be when you are only twenty and your husband has denounced you as a barefaced liar with the confetti still clinging to his hair. 'This isn't what I had in mind,' I yelled into my pillow. And I suppose it's what I have been yelling into my pillow ever since.

I blame myself. It was my deceit that took us to the altar but even so, someone should have warned me. Someone should have said: 'Expect nothing.' If you expect nothing you can build. With expectations you can only demolish and we began demolishing the minute we hit the bridal suite, if you can call a spartan cell five feet by four a suite. It was as suite as aloes.

The tragedy of marriage is that you never know what you're getting. The joke is that you always think you do. When I married George I thought I was getting the most desirable man in Southwest London. I thought his body was enough.

Looking at him now it's hard to believe, but I remember it well. And so does Jennifer, who was my bridesmaid and who has remained my closest friend. She likes to remind me of it from time to time as she wipes the tears of mirth from her wrinkles. She likes to talk about my stupidity, my ignorance, my immaturity and my lies. It gives her pleasure. But even she admits that ten years ago George Wood was a very attractive proposition.

He dressed like someone out of the *The Great Gatsby* – expensively and in fine style. He was tall and lean and blond and he had a smile that left normal women speechless, though it had the opposite effect on me. When George smiled at me I opened my mouth to speak and didn't stop until someone hit me or forced liquid between my lips. And he was the only courteous man I had ever met, view marriage. His manners were exceptional, not obvious or ingratiating but casual and natural. He had an endearing way of leaning forward to listen to what I was saying, which I can now put down to deafness, and a soppy grin he reserved for me, which I then put down to love.

I didn't care that he played rugby every Sunday and expected me to stand under an umbrella on the sidelines turning blue while he sweated in scrums so passionate I had to look away. I felt honoured. And I didn't care that he spoke so rarely there were people who thought he was mute. I liked his silences. I filled them.

He must have said something sometimes. He must have said, 'Back row or stalls?' and, 'Spaghetti or curry?' because we spent a lot of time at the cinema and in reasonably priced restaurants. But other than that, I don't know. He must have told me he was a draughtsman because I knew that's what he was, though I didn't know what *it* was.

I forgave him for living at home with his parents because I decided they were rich folk on hard times, who needed their son at home. They seemed genteel, if a little distant, even though his mother had just taken a job managing a dress shop. His father was one of those pink-and-brown men who blended with the upholstery, where he remains to this day.

It's extraordinary when you think of it, and a tribute to the power of lust, that it single-handedly transformed George's mother into a harmless gentlewoman. But the truth about marrying for lust is that you can't unless you believe it's passion and passion is blinder than love. I passionately believed that I was marrying a strong, charming, intelligent man with nice parents and good prospects who was also the most desirable man on earth. Lazy, stupid, selfish, moron — these words weren't part of my vocabulary for George. He was the man of my dreams.

I'm not entirely sure what I was to him. I know what I told him I was. I told him I was an actress who was 'resting' and that I supported myself as a waitress in a wine bar — which was true except I had never set foot on a stage in my life. I wasn't bothered by the dishonesty. I had told much worse lies in far trickier situations.

'I mean, I might be starting out,' I said to Jennifer. 'And if I intend to act but haven't actually started, then I'm an actress, aren't I?'

'No,' she said. 'You are a liar and your past will soon catch up with you.' Jennifer never beat about the bush. She still doesn't and I consider this to be one of her major faults.

I also told George that I could speak Russian, that I had three A-levels and that if ever I could abandon my art I would go to university and become a linguist. I indicated that I was not only a girl with a massive talent up her sleeve but one whose life had direction, in fact two directions, and whether I became a star of stage, screen or the Russian Embassy was entirely up to me. The reality was that I had no direction at all. I was drifting aimlessly and frivolously from one dead-end job to another, trailing behind me a single O-level in Religious Education.

I don't know why I lied. I like to think it was the strain of so many silences. But I lied a lot anyway, usually to people I thought I would never see again because I liked to give them exotic memories. It was habit, I suppose, and a need to look more adequate than I was. George was taken by my glossy veneer and I wanted to suggest something of quality underneath.

I prattled on about rep, auditions and drama schools without ever being challenged. I even spoke a smattering of Russian to him, which was a lot of sounds resembling 'ivanovitch' crammed around the word 'GUM' which I thought meant 'shop'.

I wasn't worried about anyone blowing my cover. Jennifer said unless I told George the truth before we made the vestry, she would, but I told her if she uttered a single truth in his direction I would smash everything on the inventory. This meant a lot to her because she was the keyholder to the flat and she was forced to agree discretion was the better part of squalor. 'Look,' I told her, 'they are only details. I *will* tell him, but not yet.'

My family presented no problems. They lived two hundred miles from London and George only met them once before the week of the wedding. Then the last thing my father wanted to talk about was my extremely lack lustre career. He only wanted to talk about my age, which I had admitted freely and George's age, which was twenty-two, and the folly of acting in haste. My mother had very little to say to George and not much more to say to me.

Before we headed back to London she took me aside and having established I wasn't 'in trouble', said, 'There's nothing you want to tell me, is there Tessa?' 'No,' I said. She said, 'It's a very big step,' and I said, 'For heavens sake.' I suppose she was trying to warn me. But warnings from mothers never count.

She knew I would marry if I wanted to and she didn't try to stop me. George's mother, on the other hand, fought tooth and nail, though I didn't know it at the time. She didn't just want a daughter-in-law with A-levels, she wanted a Ph.D., land and some silver in the family. She didn't just want us to wait, she wanted me dead, or at least in an irreversible coma.

I still wonder at the strength George must have produced to withstand her. The woman has the power of an Arctic icebreaker. I can only assume that he was desperate, terrified of being stuck in the bedroom next to hers forever.

Anyway, the upshot of his desperation was that he proposed eight weeks after we met and we married a month later since he couldn't see any point in hanging about. I had a feeling he thought it made sense economically but I suppressed it because it didn't suit the image I had so generously created. I married him because I thought I adored him and because I had nothing else to do.

That's how it came about that two illusions sat opposite each other on twin beds in a small hotel in Victoria on their wedding night, believing themselves to be in love, and admitted to each other they had a confession to make.

Perhaps it was the room. It was an unpretentious room in honest shades of blue and brown that froze any jubilation which might have been left over from the wedding. It could have been its starkness which led us to bare our souls before we bared our bodies.

As I twiddled with the loose knob on the drawer in the bedside table I tried to imagine what George could possibly have to confess.

'My God,' I remember thinking. 'He's going to tell me he is only half a man.' I composed myself to say I would stand by him and read books on the subject.

'You first,' he said. So I told him I wasn't an actress but just a waitress, that I didn't have three A-levels but a good solid 'O' in RE and the only Russian word I knew was 'GUM'.

'I'm sorry,' I said. I waited for him to laugh affectionately, to kiss me lightly, then fall upon me hungrily. Instead he gaped at me unattractively, plainly devastated by a blow which seemed to hit him bang in the middle of a principle I had never considered.

'So you lied,' he said. 'Why did you? I hate lies. I hate them more than anything!'

13

'Then don't think of them as lies,' I suggested, picking at strands of navy candlewick. 'Call them embellishments.'

'You deceived me,' he said, and I heard for the first time a flat nasal twang to his voice that I now know signals a sinus attack brought on by tension and candlewick.

'There's no need to sulk about it,' I said. 'It can't be that important. I'm still the same person only not an actress or Russian-speaking or with A-levels.'

'You're not the same person,' he said. 'Liars are liars.' I began to cry. I was only twenty after all and it had been a long and exhausting day. He wasn't the man I thought he was either. He was petty . . . and honest; two things I'd never been.

I threw myself face down on the bed and waited for him to pass me a large, white monogrammed handkerchief but after a few minutes it was clear he wasn't going to bother. I could hear him pacing around the room wondering if it was too late to cash in the tickets to Barcelona. Rather than wipe my nose on the bedspread or on the sleeve of my expensive going-away jumper, I groped my way to the loo and there thought, 'Sod him.'

'What were you going to tell me, then?' I shouted. 'That there was a terrible accident when you were born?' He didn't say anything. I could hear his engines revving as he prepared to take off so I rushed from the loo and threw myself at him. It wasn't very dignified and I wouldn't do it now, but it worked.

He didn't know what to do with me apart from console me so he consoled me. It wasn't until some time later that I said again, 'What were you going to tell me?'

'It seems stupid now,' he said. 'I was going to ask you to give up the stage.'

14

'What do you mean, give it up?' I asked, sitting up suddenly, anger welling in my fairly naked bosom.

'I mean, give it up,' he said. 'I wouldn't want an actress for a wife. It would be no life for me and the children.'

'Hang on,' I said. 'Hang on. It's a bit late for that, isn't it? You've already married me.'

'You what?' he replied.

'I may be your wife,' I said. 'But you've got no right to ask me to give up a career. If I want to be an actress, I will be.'

'You're not though.' he said.

'That's not the point,' I yelled. 'You should have offered me the choice when I seemed to be.' He leapt out of bed in aggravation, remembered he was naked and leapt back in again. I hooted with scorn. 'You've got nothing to hide,' I shrieked. 'I wouldn't worry about modesty.'

'Shut up,' he whispered. 'Shut up.'

'I know I'm not an actress but you thought I was. I wouldn't have asked you to give up being a draughtsman on our wedding night, and draughtsmen are nothing.'

He scrambled across to the other bed and pulled the blankets up over his head. 'Oh, God,' he said. 'This has been an awful mistake.' I burst into tears again. 'Some wedding night,' he sighed. Then he scrambled back to my bed.

'Look,' he said. 'It's all right. We're both tired. Don't cry. We'll talk about it in the morning.' And after a while I stopped crying and a while after that I lay there, wide awake, praying to the mournful tune of his eustacean tubes.

It wasn't a good beginning. But there was no changing it. It was the only beginning we had and our marriage took off from there, skidding wildly all over the place.

CHAPTER TWO

Heated Moments

Poor old George didn't know what hit him. There he was, an easy-going man, spoilt by twenty-two years in the shadow of his mother's pointed hat, never having been called upon to utter anything other than a polite response, never having had to deal with any emotions other than those expressed by the eyebrows, with only a few words of English at his disposal, suddenly alone in a foreign part with a bride he didn't recognize.

And if that wasn't enough, on the seventh day someone robbed him of his most prized possession. He would willingly have traded me for its safe return. As he informed the police in Barcelona twenty miles away in a single agonized shout, it was worth two hundred quid.

I wasn't at my best on the honeymoon. I was in deep shock, thrashing about in an anticlimax which was suffocating. Not only was my husband a man who could ask his beautiful, talented wife to give up a promising stage career, he was a man who didn't recognize an internal struggle, even when it was regurgitated at his feet.

The most shattering thing about George, I discovered on our honeymoon, was his serious reluctance to react to anything other than the food put in front of him and the sight of my barely clad flesh. He didn't want to know about inner torment, and I was being torn apart in the darkest recesses of my being. He had wrenched me from my mother's bosom before I'd had time to say goodbye to the last of my childhood.

I wanted him to prove that he could take my mother's place, that he loved me as much and was as strong, as capable and as fascinated by the small print of my everyday worries. I wanted him to be as sure, as stable, as forgiving and as permanent. And I wanted him to show it.

But he wasn't interested in everyday worries. Until he met me he didn't have any. I became a very, very big one and I put a lot of energy into making him deal with me, even though the sun was shining and the Hotel Ricardo was paradise despite the plumbing.

I threw tantrum after tantrum to provoke magnificent displays of courage, passion, manhood, wisdom and love, willing him to be the man I had invented inside his beautiful, silent shell. But he stood there aghast, unable to act. He accused me of being childish. He asked what had happened to my happy old self. He said this wasn't the girl he knew.

'Knew!' I screamed at him from the bidet where I was rinsing underwear. 'Knew! You don't and never did know me.'

'I'm beginning to,' he declared with dull precision.

Why I waited until the honeymoon to look for the man within the man I still don't know. Most people jockey for starting positions before they hurl themselves through the marital barrier. At least they enjoy the odd wrangle in the paddock. But we didn't

In the heady days of our courtship the only provocative things I said were of a seedy nature, which appealed to the seed in George, and I was so entranced by the fine lines of his profile and of his biceps that I allowed myself to think I was getting a silent tower of strength.

Within days of our marriage I had to admit to myself that he was a leaning tower and the direction in which he leant was away from me. On the third night we stood miserably on our balcony with its half sea view, locked in a desperate stalemate.

'Where is the honey?' I said to George.

'Where is the moon?' he replied.

It was clear that our voyage of discovery, our embarkation on life's great passage, the celebration of our union in the privacy of a faraway place on a Thomson's package was hanging in ruins. And we had twelve more days to go. Someone had to do something.

I tried to see how we might survive. I tried to look at it rationally, but I couldn't see beyond my urgent need to make George into something he apparently was not. I couldn't believe I had married a nonreactor of such nuclear proportions. I couldn't believe my judgement had been so poor. I thought he only needed working on.

By blocking the best efforts of my most effective weapons, which are spite and pathos, George drove me to reach for something more powerful: I reached for the brass letter-opener I had bought for my father from the souvenir shop in the lobby and thought about what it might do to the vacant expression in his lush, blue eyes, which suggested that he was tired and that he'd been tricked.

If he said it once he said it a hundred times during our first three days: 'I don't know what you're talking about.' Either he didn't know what I was talking about, or he did but didn't want to talk about it.

He didn't want to talk about the things he'd said on our wedding night we would talk about in the morning. He said it would be best if we put it behind us. And I, delighted to round things off neatly, replied,

'Good idea. They weren't very big lies anyway.' But he said he didn't know about that. Lies were lies.

'I can't pretend you didn't lie to me, Tessa,' he said. 'You did and that's that. I simply don't see any point in talking about it ever again.'

It isn't in my nature not to talk about things, let alone ever again. If I don't discuss things I fester and contaminate everyone within spitting distance. George failed to understand on our honeymoon that unless we resolved things and resolved things quickly, life would rapidly come to resemble the infection unit in a snake-bite ward. He could live with things unresolved just by chalking up black marks. I could only operate with a clean slate.

I abandoned the idea of the letter-opener because I couldn't bear to see a goodlooking man wasted. But I began to work harder on my tantrums, urging him to understand their point and to tell me that, anyway, he hadn't married me for my scrupulous honesty and that we did have more in common than an interest in each other's bodies. Instead he said, 'Do you want to go home?'

On the third night I was inspired by some small voice from a distant melodrama that I'd stored away for future use. By the third night, when the tantrums were clearly getting us nowhere, I took up fainting. Not only was fainting less exhausting, it was more graceful.

It began as an instinctive reaction to yet another bitter blow. George, plodding across my finer feelings, as we sipped the Hotel Ricardo's killer sangria, said he didn't see any point in a romantic trip into the hills when we could use the money to buy duty-free brandy at Gatwick. He said, 'Seen one hill, seen them all.' As we waited for our main course I stared at him with deep hurt and mortification, then, without a murmur, slid carefully under the table.

21

It wasn't very comfortable but it was interesting. The waiter arrived with the chicken and chips just as I hit the floor and I was able to see beneath my lashes that he stared at me with wonderment. I heard George push out his chair and stagger to his feet to come and have a stare as well. He didn't as I'd hoped he might, fling himself on to my breast to check my heart beat or scream for emergency services.

'I'm sorry,' I heard him say to the waiter. 'I think my wife has fainted.' He crawled around to my side of the table to peer at me. 'Yes, she's fainted,' he confirmed.

The waiter also dropped to his knees to peer at me. I moaned gently. 'She'll be all right, won't you Tessa?' George called. He tugged at my shoulder. I waved my arm in what I hoped was a fair imitation of someone returning to consciousness and whacked him hard in the mouth. Then I opened my eyes. He helped me to my feet.

'What happened?' I asked.

'I don't know,' he said, rubbing his jaw with a suggestion of suspicion that I bitterly resented.

'I fainted,' I said, and to get rid of the suspicion added, 'I think I'm going to be sick.'

'The ladies is behind the palm,' he cried in alarm and shoved me in that general direction.

'No,' I cried back. 'I want to go to our room.'

'Yes, of course,' he said, remembering his manners. And with hardly a backward glance at the chicken and chips he guided me gingerly to the lift.

It caused quite a stir in the dining-room. People wondered, I suppose, if I was pregnant or had a tumour and looked concerned. George took his cue from them. He helped me into bed and after half an hour or so of his quite pleasant attentions I felt well enough to order food from room service.

'What caused it?' he asked manfully.

'I don't know,' I said. 'Too much sun, I suppose.'

'Then tomorrow we'll go to the mountains,' he said. I didn't smirk and if I smiled it was with relief that our marriage might be saved after all and that he had a heart that could be reached.

On the seventh day he astonished me by displaying a passion so fierce I could scarcely credit. Someone pinched his camera as we lay amid the oil-slicks savouring the return of civilized conduct.

'Someone's nicked my camera,' he yelled. 'It's worth two hundred quid.'

To another couple such a calamity might have been a unifying experience. But to George and me the theft only underlined our essential differences, the most essential of which was that I didn't give a fig about his camera.

Of course I was sorry about it. But I wasn't prepared to suffer for it. As far as he knew I was not a well person, fainting as I seemed to be doing a couple of times a day from the effects of the sun and not getting my own way. But this he forgot in his despair. 'Do something,' he yelled at me. 'My mother gave it to me. Don't just lie there.'

'Are you sure?' I asked purposefully. 'It could be under a sandal or something.'

'It isn't under anything,' he bellowed. 'Some rotten thief has made off with it.' He began striding up the beach looking for a posse and a hangman to see justice done. I hung back in case he decided to strip-search the first shady character he clapped eyes on. And I tried to calm him.

'It's covered by insurance,' I called. 'You'll get your money back.'

'What's that got to do with it?' he snarled. I caught up with him and grabbed his arm to indicate a certain solidarity, though it was obvious to me he was mad. But he shook me off, offending me terribly. I thought about fainting but my sense of timing prevailed.

23

'Where are you going?' I panted. He didn't bother to answer. 'Why don't we report it to reception? They can call the police.' But he headed down the main road and up some back streets to the police station, which he found with the same instinct mothers use to find public lavatories.

The small Spanish policeman, with even less command of the language than George, took a few details and looked at us forlornly. He shrugged his shoulders unhappily at George's fury. I winked at him to show I was impartial. This was a mistake. George said. 'What did you do that for?'

'What?' I asked.

'Wink. What did you wink at him for? This isn't a bloody joke, Tessa. I'm the victim of a crime.'

'I didn't,' I said.

'I saw you,' he said. Then off he strode again, the unhappy husband of a harlot liar, whom he probably believed had conspired to have him robbed. As I made my own way back to the hotel I realized he had such a low opinion of my honesty that he was capable of believing I had stolen his rotten camera.

I found him fuming on the bed and wished he was fuming for me. 'It's only a camera,' I said.

'It was *my* camera,' he replied.

This was the point, the essential difference. I thought and still think everything is replaceable. He thought and still thinks nothing is. He thinks once you own something it becomes unique because it's yours. He attaches a mystical importance to ownership that I don't understand.

'Of course you don't understand theft,' he spat from the pillow. 'You're basically dishonest.' This led me to faint, not to win his attention but to escape from it.

It was a very hot day, I remember, and the sun cut across the end of the bed and into my eyes as I lay on the white-tiled floor waiting for him to come and

24

revive me. I waited and waited but he had withdrawn his heart. I lay there alone, wishing I hadn't fainted, wondering if I would have to pretend all my life and quietly trying to decide who would speak first. He did.

'Get up, Tessa,' he said. 'You look silly. You know there's nothing wrong with you.' I thought about it. 'Come on,' he urged. 'Get up.' I tried to decipher his tone but couldn't. I had to get up, I realized, because he'd called my bluff. However, I felt a bit daft.

'We have to sort things out, don't we,' he said. He came over and pulled me to my feet and led me out on to the balcony.

'Oh, George,' I said, relieved that he was speaking of his own accord and trying the phrase on for size. I fervently hoped he would put the fainting behind us and never discuss it again.

'Tell me what's the matter with you,' he said.

It was on the tip of my tongue to say disappointment, which would have been true but I couldn't. I didn't want to hurt him any more than he had already been hurt by his tragic loss. 'Fear,' I said pathetically. It was more captivating and not far off the mark.

'There's nothing to be frightened of,' he said. 'We're married.' We gazed across the rusty headland and looked out to sea where the future looked hazy and I thought that of all the things he might have said, that was the least comforting. But I was deeply moved that he'd said anything at all.

It wasn't just fear I was suffering from. It was dread of the future and regret for the past which was gone forever, grief for a finished chapter which was now a memory. I was too young for memories. George wasn't my mother and had none of her qualities. I was going to have to learn to live without them.

I looked at him watching the beach and wondered if he was pining for his camera. I thought, I'll have to teach him to love me as he loved it. Would it be worth it, I wondered. What, after all, did he have going for him?

It was a silly thing to ask myself because what he had going for him was as plain as the nose on his face. It was the nose on his face and the rest of his face and his neck and shoulders and everything underneath them. My mother had nothing to match it.

CHAPTER THREE

The Bosom of His Family

There's nothing natural about marriage. There's nothing natural about two people trying to live together in harmony forever despite insuperable odds. It's probably man's least natural state.

George's and my marriage was even more unnatural than most because of the sheer size of our insuperable odd. Some people quite like Mrs Wood but she looms large in my memory of our early married life. She must be the biggest odd ever seen in the history of domestic bliss.

The reason we set up house two blocks away from her in Mrs Maitland's upstairs flat wasn't because she had bullied Mrs Maitland into giving us a pound a week off the rent. It was because George couldn't bear to be parted from her. I wasn't the only one looking for a mother figure when I married. George was too. I have come to believe that everyone is: we marry to replace our ageing mothers and we marry people of the opposite sex as a cover.

George wanted me to be his mother. He wanted me to pick up the threads of his home life where she had left off. After a month I said, 'If I pay the extra pound, can we move?'

'No,' he said. 'We'd starve.' His faith in my ability to

get edible food on the table was at such a low ebb after a month that we were eating with his parents five times a week, twice on Sundays. On the scale laid down by the Eurovision Song Contest, he rated my ability as a homemaker somewhere around Norway.

'A man needs one hot meal a day,' he said. This was the sort of rubbish he'd had drilled into him from birth which, at the age of twenty-two, despite his marriage to a woman better out of the kitchen than in, he saw little point in questioning.

It took me only a short time to realize that when you take on someone for life you're taking on their past, and George's past was his mother. Whatever he may have been at birth – and I'm perfectly prepared to believe that at birth he had something going for him – had been squelched within her terrible will and bent to her insane specifications.

She turned George into the sort of mindless creep who believes all women can cook, wash, clean, sew, iron, shop and skivvy with the same skill, which comes to them naturally, like periods. He was shattered to find that in anything to do with housekeeping I was as hopeless as he was.

This wasn't because my past in any way resembled his. It was simply because I wasn't interested. My past was riddled with domestic experience. My mother believed her children were ablebodied and should pull their weight. When I left home at eighteen I knew enough about household management to know it was bottom of my list of fascinating ways to spend my time.

Because George had never lived away from home, housework didn't feature on his list at all. He'd never been known to lay a hand on a tea towel because his mother believed the kitchen was no place for a man.

'Why isn't it?' I said to George.

'I don't know,' he replied. He isn't a questioning

29

man and he wasn't prepared to argue about it. All he wanted was to have something hot on the table when he came home from work and I wasn't that something. It had to have gravy over it.

'Gravy!' I cried when he pointed this out after a week of carefully arranged salads. 'What gravy?'

'The gravy you get on food,' he said.

'You don't put gravy on salads,' I said. 'Or grills.'

'My mother does,' he said.

This is the sort of woman George's mother is. She puts gravy on grills.

'If you want gravy on your grill,' I said, 'you had better go home to get it.' So he did, taking me with him, parading me before her three times a week and twice on Sundays as someone who had failed to meet the standard she had set for serving George. She put gravy on her grills, I discovered, to disguise them. Underneath the gravy was polystyrene.

Of course things are different now. Now I get on with Mrs Wood like a house burning down. But then, she was like a mischievous match darting from one corner of our tinder-box relationship to another. I blame her for the cross-purposes George and I were mainly at. You have to blame someone.

I can honestly say she didn't welcome me into the bosom of her family as the daughter she never had. She made it clear from the very beginning she didn't see much future in the arrangement I had with her son. She might have been happier with a daughter-in-law less partial to black leather, silver nail polish and nights on the tiles, but probably not. She just wasn't prepared to give him up after only twenty-two years, at least not to another woman. I don't think she felt she'd had her money's worth.

Certainly she didn't take seriously the claim I had on him, despite what we'd said at the church and in front of witnesses. When we came back from our honeymoon the first thing she said to George was in horror. 'You look exhausted, dear!' she gasped. 'What have you been up to?'

'What did she expect?' I hissed when she left us briefly to get him an aspirin. 'We didn't go away to sleep.'

I should have protested immediately at her presence in the marriage but she was like one of those mad people who sits next to you on the bus. You don't know until it's too late that you should have moved, and suddenly you can't because it's too embarrassing.

However, the more I was thrown together with her in her kitchen across the interminable mounds of washing-up, the more resentful I became. She talked to me as little as possible and when she did it was to tell me how to make the most of George's life. 'He loves Continental food,' she said. 'I expect you know that.'

'French fries,' I said. 'We live off them.'

She told me I was going to have to be very clever to work and run the flat but she was sure I could manage as she was now managing, even though I was very young. 'I won't be doing any running,' I assured her. 'I'm incredibly lazy.' Stalagmites appeared from nowhere between her teeth.

I didn't actually see why the general tone of our life should change just because we now lived together as man and wife. I'd made the one major concession I thought was necessary. I'd taken a job in an estate agent's office where I was able to use my meagre typing to give George the decent sort of wife he'd had in mind when he'd rejected the actress. It was nine-to-five and solid and without glamour and boring. And badly paid, considering the sacrifice.

Take-aways still featured prominently in my idea of a sensible diet, and tear-away nights out seemed to me to be the only fit reward for days of paralysing monotony. I didn't even want to tear away very far,

31

only to the pictures, or to the parties our unmarried friends still gave, or even to the pub. But George wanted our life to be a married one, by which he meant like his mother's and father's. He wanted me to be a wife and him to be a husband.

His mother agreed with him. After a few weeks it seemed to me I was being thoroughly exposed to her so I could learn to be her. I thought they were trying to brainwash me.

Liberation didn't come into it. I didn't want to be liberated. I was still in the grips of passion. What's liberated, anyway, when you're trapped in your mother-in-law's web? The problem was status. In George's eyes I was only assistant to his mother. It was far more important to me to rid myself of her than of the demands made by my husband. The only way to get rid of her was to prove she was superfluous. So I bought a duvet.

This mightn't seem like a mighty blow for freedom but it was. I chucked into the depths of an iron chest all the linen sheets and pure wool blankets she knew could destroy my life which she'd given in spite and I hid the key. 'Why?' George asked. 'They were perfectly good sheets and blankets.'

'This is a perfectly good duvet,' I said. 'I saved for it. It will save making the bed in the morning, it will save ironing the sheets and it will save dry-cleaning the blankets. It is a very saving thing.'

There wasn't much he could say in the face of so much thrift. 'I see,' he said. I was delighted. Although Mrs Wood still lurked around the curtains she had provided and in the kitchen cupboards, I had swept her from my bed. That night as I lay snuggled in his elbow, I said to George, 'You don't know what it means to me, not sleeping with your mother.'

He said, 'This thing smells like cardboard and my arm has gone to sleep.'

My pleasure lasted until the first time we had to change the cover. The occasion of its removal is embossed on my understanding of the man George is and is a landmark in our relationship.

'We can't even make a bed together,' I said bitterly, and added for good measure, 'You are a clumsy fool.'

'We had mastered sheets and blankets,' he replied stonily, and out he stormed leaving me with the wrecked bedclothes and a splintered truce. I had bought the duvet the day after we had resolved the laundry crisis. Now we were having the laundry crisis all over again. If I'd known then what I know now the tragedy could have been avoided: two stupid people cannot put a duvet into its cover together. Trying to do so can put a strain on any relationship.

The laundry crisis was a slow-burning thing. It came to a head when I told him that I wouldn't do his ironing because I had never done Jennifer's. 'You weren't married to Jennifer,' he said, bewildered.

'So what?' I replied.

'My mother never quibbled over it,' he said. 'I don't understand you.' This was George's problem. His single experience of women, apart from the dozens who had thrown themselves into his hot embrace and out again, was her.

I pointed this out somewhere along the A23 because we were going to Brighton for the day to enjoy ourselves. I said his mother's attitude to life was nauseating in the extreme. I accused him of conspiring. I said I wouldn't do his ridiculous laundry. I said in India they burnt unwanted brides and I would save him the trouble.

As he grappled with the steering of his mighty Morris Minor I threw the map in his face and opened the door, threatening to throw myself into the road. We were travelling at about thirty miles per hour, I suppose. Top speed, anyway.

There was a demented flurry as he tried to shake the map from his head, grab for me and hold the wheel. He screamed, 'Tessa, get back, you fool.'

'I can't take any more,' I cried. 'I didn't marry for the laundry.'

'I will do the laundry,' he said. So I got back in, closed the door and we had a very nice day at the seaside. But the duvet ruined everything. Rather than hurl himself into the struggle that was necessary to master three ounces of polyester fibre, rather than try again to pull it into its cover with a small amount of thinking and teamwork, George went home to his mother. I would never have gone home to my mother. It would have been demeaning. I phoned Jennifer.

I told her George had left me. I said he'd been lured away by his evil mother and gravy. She said to come to the pictures and forget about it. I said, 'Jennifer, you don't understand married life.' She said, should she come round and boil kettles or something. I said she couldn't. He might come back.

'OK,' she said. 'Suffer on your own, then.' So I did. I sat at home with a bottle of rum and tried to look as if I was drinking myself to death in his absence.

It was very dull because he was gone all afternoon and well into the night. I packed my bags and upacked them twice. I emptied his drawers all over the bedroom once and I watched the television in a state of rising hysteria. At ten o'clock I heard him coming up the stairs and I composed myself to look drunken and beautiful on the sofa. He walked in well fed and nonchalant.

'What's this?' he said, settling down in front of the telly. 'Worth watching, is it?'

'I wouldn't know,' I said. I tried to scan his jumper for gravy stains, certain that in his awful need to satisfy his craving he would have slopped it all over him. But his jumper looked spick-and-span. 'She's washed it,'

I thought. He put his arm along the back of the sofa in a pathetic attempt to make bodily contact. I moved away from it.

'I will leave in the morning,' I announced.

'Where for?' he asked.

'There will be no forwarding address,' I said.

'Oh,' he murmured. Then he said, 'There's no need, you know.'

'Why?' I asked. 'We are ruining our lives. I can't stand eating with your mother five times a week.'

'We'll stop,' he said. 'I've bought you a present. Close your eyes.' I closed them and he handed me a small, oblong box that for one insane minute I thought might contain a jewel. It was gravy powder.

'I even know how to make it,' he chortled. 'I'll be in charge of gravy.' And after that we only went to his parents once a week, and I changed the bed on my own.

This is the stuff on which marriages are built; powdery sort of stuff that goes lumpy at the drop of a hat. Marriage is as natural as Bisto.

CHAPTER FOUR

Home Truths

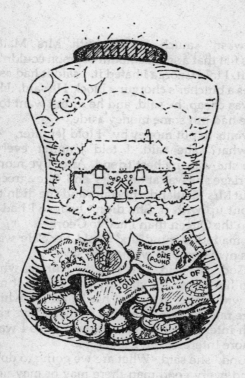

There wasn't much wrong with Mrs Maitland's upstairs flat that a small amount of arson couldn't cure. I hated it. I told George I hated it. I said it had as much charm as a butcher's chopping block. He said, 'I know.' But it was cheap, he said, and he didn't want to move until we had put some money aside.

'He wants to put money by,' I told Jennifer.

'By what?' she said. I told Jennifer everything because she was my best friend. After five months of my marriage she was at her wits' end. She agreed with me about Mrs Maitland's upstairs and she didn't know why I put up with it. She didn't believe I had easier access to the Queen than I had to George.

'He's made his mind up,' I told her. 'He wants to own his own home so we have to save.'

'Oh, God,' she said. This was the Jennifer who later clung to her house for stability and hid in it making things with toilet rolls for her children while her marriage raged around her. But in those days she was as much interested in home-ownership as I was, and I was more interested in Esperanto.

'Oh, God,' she said. 'What are we going to do?'

Behind every good man there may or may not be a woman. But behind every faint-hearted wife there is always a best friend. Jennifer has been behind me for as long as I've known her, pushing. I'm not complaining. Without her I'd probably still be in Mrs Maitland's upstairs with a Safeways bag over my head.

It's a tricky business, however, staying married and keeping a best friend. George and Jennifer have never thought much of each other, which is understandable given the things I've told them. George doesn't like Jennifer's influence. I say she has no influence. He says: 'Do termites have influence?' He has never forgiven her for our first public rift. He says it was all her fault. I've told him many times it wouldn't have happened if he hadn't been so stingy about the rent.

When I say public I mean involving others. We'd often fallen out in front of others but not with others joining in and hitting each other.

I could just as easily blame George's friend Michael Davis but George says he doesn't remember Michael Davis being there. This is a lie. He knows as well as I do that Michael Davis was there but he went off Michael Davis that night and not long after it he stopped playing rugby with him, and not long after that he began saying, 'Michael who?' But Michael Davis was as much to blame as anyone except Jennifer who, to be frank, did slightly overplay her hand.

I don't think she meant to. I think her cup sort of ranneth over. She acted on the spur of the moment because the mood was right, the opportunity was there and she'd had too much to drink. The next day when she rang to tell me she had a black eye, she said I should never have involved her in a private matter. I said, 'Jennifer, it was you who made it public. I told you everything in confidence.'

She said, 'Thanks very much. I'll never try to help you again.'

I said, 'That's fine by me.' The result of her help was that, whereas the day before I'd had a best friend and a husband who preferred me to a festering carcass, suddenly I had neither. 'Never again,' I vowed. 'Never again will I confide to anyone a single detail of my marriage that can be used in evidence against me.' I meant it at the time.

I was horrified by her indiscretion. When she had said, 'What can we do?' I hadn't for a minute thought she would offer the question for public debate the first opportunity she had. If I'd known she was going to I would never have asked her to bring her boyfriend round and George would never have invited Michael Davis, who came with a girl he met on the train. We'd have settled for another early night. God knows I was getting used to them.

The evening began well enough. I remember the exhilaration with which I greeted everyone and how chirpily I apologized for the smell of Mrs Maitland's newly acquired tom. There weren't enough chairs and everyone threw themselves to the floor while George poured wine in the kitchen.

We were smiling mindlessly at each other when he arrived with his tray and said, also smiling, 'What's wrong with the chairs?' It was his tidy mind.

'Fleas,' I said. 'Michael says he saw a flea.' George looked startled.

Michael said quickly, 'Only a small one.' Then, realizing George was unamused, said, 'Not really,' and heaved himself heavily into the armchair to prove he hadn't. Its back fell off. Everyone laughed hysterically, from exhilaration I suppose, but George said, 'Oh, no!'

Michael stopped laughing first because he was the first to notice George's tight little mouth. 'I'm really sorry,' he said, as he scrambled to his feet. 'I'll buy you a new one.'

'Don't be silly,' I said. 'It came off a skip.'

'It didn't,' snapped George, trying to force it together again. 'You know it was Mrs Maitland's mother's.'

Peter, Jennifer's boyfriend – a man rising rapidly in stationery without the benefit of a sense of humour – said to lighten the tone, 'I like skips.'

The girl off the train, whose name I think was Wimpy, remarked, 'Yuk, he's bleeding.'

George said, 'It was a perfectly good chair. Tessa is in a vile mood.'

'I'm not,' I yelled. But no one seemed to believe me.

Jennifer said next day that obviously I had begun the evening looking for a fight. She said everything I said was designed to rattle George. I said, 'That's not true. I was being joyful.'

She said, 'Joyful as in crematorium.'

I said, 'Whose friend are you? If you think about it, it was George who was getting at me.' If he hadn't been getting at me precisely he was certainly watching me very carefully. He had for some weeks been showing signs of finding me less than wildly funny in public.

He had started to accuse me of showing-off and to issue warnings before we left the flat. 'Don't go over the top tonight,' he would say. Where once he'd been the first to laugh and refill my glass, he was suddenly the only person frowning and looking as if he might throw-up. His disapproval only made me slightly uneasy. Instead of showing-off centre stage where I usually functioned, I became sly. I caused monumental diversions in the wings and I sniped.

I suppose I was sniping that night about the flat because I was ashamed of it and because Michael Davis made it easy. 'Been here long?' he asked, when the remains of the chair had been carefully buried under the bed.

'We've only been married six months,' George said. 'We're saving for a house.'

'George has his eye on the Palace,' I said. 'We'll stay here until we can afford it.'

'Oh,' said Michael.

'No, it will be worth it,' I insisted. 'Seventy-eight years being blinded by yellow ochre and formica for a few months in a place we can call our own.'

'Don't you like it here?' asked Scrumpy.

'It does while we're saving,' muttered George. Jennifer threw me a look of serious significance which I couldn't quite make out but she said nothing. She waited until we'd finished eating a vile sludge of pasta and lumpy bits, then while everyone was trying to come to terms with their digestion, she dive-bombed.

'Why are you being such a pig, George?' she said. 'Why don't you move from here when you know Tessa hates it?'

'Pardon?' said George. He looked at Jennifer as if she'd attacked his mother, which she had, since Mrs Maitland's upstairs was her idea.

'You can't be in love with the place,' she said. 'Let's face it. It's a dump.' George turned to me wordlessly for support, reeling under the attack which he had not provoked as far as he could see. But I sat there smiling like Mother Teresa, fascinated.

'Look at it,' Jennifer said calmly. 'It's poky, the furniture is horrible. There's nothing in it that looks like Tessa apart from the underwear in the bathroom.'

No one could interrupt. We were all too frightened. 'It's in a nasty little back street in a pointless suburb where she's cut off from all her friends. She's going round the bend out here. You'll have to move.'

I thought he was going to haemorrhage. He could barely speak. He looked at Jennifer. He looked at me. He looked at Michael Davis. Then he stood up and grabbed the pepper mill. I froze.

'Drop dead, Jennifer,' he said. 'It's none of your business where we live.'

'Lord,' I thought. Like everyone else I was concentrating hard on the tablecloth, staggered by both of them. I had never seen George so offended. I thought I should say something but so did everyone else. Peter thought he should speak on behalf of the bridesmaid.

'Just a minute, George,' he said. 'You can't talk to Jennifer like that. It mightn't be her business but she is Tessa's oldest friend and she might have a point.'

'Of course I have a point,' said Jennifer. 'Tessa's happiness. George shouldn't need me to mention it.'

'What I think about Tessa's happiness has nothing to do with you,' he said. 'It's my business and Tessa's business, though this doesn't seem to have occurred to Tessa.' He glared at me. I ducked in case he threw the pepper mill.

Thumper said, 'I think it's a horrible flat. I wouldn't live here. It smells like dead cat.'

Michael didn't move for fear of breaking another chair but his eyes bulged sideways in his anxiety to leap to George's defence. He said, 'What's it got to do with you, fatty'

This was unkind. She was a short, bleached girl with a pancake expression and fluorescent lips that wanted to crawl down her chin, but she wasn't fat. I thought she had a mind like a razor.

'I'm entitled to my opinion,' she said. 'I wouldn't live here if you paid me.'

'There,' said Jennifer.

'I'm sorry,' Michael shouted. 'I'm sorry, but you are all out of your brains. You've got no right. Attacking another man's home. None of you knows how to behave. You are a load of rude, ungrateful cretins.' This lead to many people jumping to their feet and several chairs collapsing in panic. Mrs Maitland downstairs knocked on the ceiling with her mop.

'Everyone sit down,' George said. 'This is ridiculous.' But no one would. They all wanted to fight each other. Michael, who hadn't liked the way Peter had

43

sniggered when he broke the chair, took the chance to jab him hard in the stomach.

'What did you do that for?' Peter yelped. Jennifer, outraged, slapped Michael's scratched hand and made it bleed again. 'Oh, yuk,' said Dumper. She picked up her handbag and gave an almighty swipe that caught both Jennifer and Michael in the face.

Mr Maitland came up and knocked on the door. He told us he couldn't hear the wrestling for the noise upstairs, so would we all pipe down or he'd tell George's mother. George said he was going out, and went.

I said I would make coffee but no one wanted any. They wanted to go home and I said probably they should. Jennifer said to me pointedly, 'Will you be all right, Tessa? Do you want to come back to the flat?' I said there was a battered wives refuge half a mile away if I needed it.

George must have waited in the garden because the minute they were out of sight he crept up the stairs. I went and hid in the bathroom. He came and banged on the door.

'Tessa,' he yelled. 'Are you in there?'

'No,' I said. 'It wasn't my fault. I was the only one who didn't say a word.'

'I don't want to see that Jennifer in this flat or anywhere else ever again. I mean it. Do you hear that? I mean it.'

'OK.' I said. What are six years of bosom friendship compared to a madman outside with a pepper mill? I came out carefully, prepared to scream for Mr Maitland to come up with the mop but George was collapsed on the sofa.

'Why did you tell her you were miserable?' he said. 'Why didn't you tell *me*?'

'I did tell you,' I said.

44

'Did you?' He sat for a while gazing at a brown stain on the yellow wallpaper. I joined him on the sofa. I felt guilty about being disloyal. I said, 'It could be quite cosy if we kept our eyes closed.'

'But the smell,' he said. 'It will never smell cosy.'

'I want to move,' I said. 'I really do, George.'

'We'll move,' he said.

And we did, closer into town to an unfurnished flat on a road near a common favoured by juggernauts. We used our savings to pay for the fixtures and fittings, which were three mock-Habitat kitchen units and a single built-in wardrobe in the bedroom. We furnished it from junk shops and with dangerous second-hand appliances and I painted a mural in the bathroom. I loved it. It was home.

But George has never really forgiven Jennifer. She is the side of my nature he doesn't trust, which I daresay is fair since I still moan to her about him all the time. He continues to see her almost as often as I do because he is not prepared to go out every time she comes in.

I didn't dare tell her he never wanted to see her again because it reeked of having to make a choice and you can't make a choice between a best friend and a husband. You just have to hope they grow used to each other. He still bans her from our lives from time to time but he knows it's useless. I need her and I'd be impossible without her.

CHAPTER FIVE

When a Wife is a Sweet Trolley

I wasn't tempted to look at Other Men until well into the second year of our marriage and then I was driven to it. I flung myself at the head of another not because it was better looking but because it spoke and I was desperate to be spoken to. I suppose I was growing up.

I wanted to debate the great mysteries of the universe, not just Life, the Cosmos and Truth but where oil came from, why I hadn't been born into royalty and what compound interest was. George didn't. 'Oh, no!' was all he had to say on such matters. Eventually he said, 'Oh, no!' once too often and there was spotty Paul Nolan waiting by my desk to whisk me off to the wine bar and heated conversation.

George's and my conversation was almost never heated. In fact we didn't have conversations. We only ever had me trying.

'Death's a funny thing, isn't it?' I might say.

'What?'

'Death. It's a funny thing. To be dead is a funny thing.'

'Right.'

'What do you think?'

'Sorry?'

'I said, what do you think about being dead?'

'Dead?'

'Dead.'

'Look, Tessa, I'm trying to drive this car through very heavy traffic and there's a maniac on my bumper and a woman in front of me.'

'Yes, but imagine it. If you can imagine you're dead you must begin to understand life. What do you think?'

'Nothing.'

George, of course, had been grown up since he was eight. At eight he was as mature as he was ever going to be. By twenty-two he had found the mould into which he wanted to set. It was a very, very quiet one. He didn't mind chatting but he didn't want to talk. He didn't mind me talking but he didn't want to reply. It was like playing tennis by yourself in an empty field.

I longed for a few rallies. Nothing fancy, just me speaking, him speaking, me speaking. But he resented questions like 'isn't it' or 'aren't they'. He met them with his limp volley and allowed them to drop into the net. 'Not now, love. I've had a long day,' he would say.

'But it's important,' I would cry. 'I want to know what you think about the Bible.'

'I don't think about the Bible.'

'You must think something. You went to Sunday school.'

'I think it's long.'

To begin with I clung to the knowledge that he must have had a brain once somewhere because he had three A-levels and eight O's. Only once did I allow myself to think his mother must have paid for them. I waited and watched for signs that it was still in working order.

I told myself it had to be because he used it every day at his office. He just switched it off when he came home because he didn't consider it a domestic appliance. He clearly didn't want to waste it on me. The pain of this explanation was enormous but it was better than admitting I had married a vegetable. I spent ages trying to get him to confess.

'Why won't you talk to me?' I would cry.

'I do talk to you,' he would reply.

'You don't. You humour me. It's because I'm not as clever as you, isn't it? Isn't it? George? Isn't it?' When he refused to meet the challenge I tried creeping up on him.

'What are you doing,' I would ask, running my fingers through his hair, 'when your mouth is shut and your eyes are open and you aren't watching television?'

'I give up,' he would yawn.

'No, really.'

'Resting,' he would say. It seemed impossible that a man so young and virile, with such a lithe and healthy body could need so much rest. I toyed with the idea that he had a wasting disease but he put on a stone when he gave up rugby. Eventually I had to face the truly terrible truth.

The reason he didn't want to talk about anything heavier than my Yorkshire pudding was that nothing concerned him more than my Yorkshire pudding. He accepted life at face value, dealt with it and moved on. He didn't want to know what caused it.

While I was beginning to regret my misspent youth and to wish I had learnt something at school, he was gliding towards early senility with a smile on his face. I was trying to crank my brain into action but he wanted to put his into Supp-Hose.

'You think too much for your own good,' he said.

'You are a moron,' I replied. That settled it. The die were cast. Having spotted him for what he was, I allowed myself to be swamped by an emotion so powerful, so irresistible that I knew things could never be the same again. It was burgeoning hate. And I was right. Things never were.

The hate has been in our marriage ever since. It's mutual. George recognized it the very minute I did, as we glared into each other's contorted features and inwardly gagged. It isn't the same as the shrill moments of frustration and irritation that rise and fall with situations. It lurks just below the surface and it can blow without warning.

I hate George as deeply as I love him only less often. When I hate him I can't bear the sight of him, the sound of him or the thought of what lies ahead. But I know how to deal with it. I go and look through his insurance policies and plan a life as a single but very beautiful mother. I imagine him dead and what I will wear to his funeral. I decide which of his friends will come to call on me when he's gone. And then I feel better. I just wait for it to pass, which it always does. Then, however, I didn't know it would. Then, I dealt with it by flinging myself at the inside of Paul Nolan's head without bothering to make my intentions clear.

Paul Nolan's head was shaped like a pineapple and his skin was like a pineapple's. But it didn't bother him and it didn't bother me. It was jam-packed with opinions and this is what drew me to him. He didn't mind listening to mine either and telling me why they were wrong.

He was obviously clever. He read books by foreign authors and knew what they meant, and he actually liked going to films with subtitles. What young wife with a blossoming brain and a log of a husband wouldn't have been fascinated?

He used to confide in me when everyone else was out of the office. He didn't want to be an estate agent at all. He wanted to be a playwright.

'I used to act,' I told him. 'I gave up the stage when I married so I could spend more time with my husband.'

51

'What a shame,' he said. 'He's a lucky man. You must love him a lot.'

'A bit,' I said. There was no point in exaggerating. With Paul Nolan I tried to be intellectually honest. You could tell he was. He told me he was. I said I could tell. I didn't try to keep my feelings from George because it would have been wrong.

'Had lunch at the wine bar with Paul Nolan. God, he's a clever man.'

'Did you?' George said. 'I had a sandwich in the pub with Mark Punnet.'

'That was nice. What did you talk about?'

'Can't remember.'

'We talked about The Theatre,' I said. He smirked.

'Did you tell him you were an actress?'

'He knows what I am,' I said. As a matter of fact, I thought he did. I thought it was pretty obvious that I was a mature married woman who enjoyed conversation and a glass of cheap wine at lunch time and who, though she considered him ugly, didn't mind being seen with him because his looks were irrelevant.

I told Jennifer that it was the most mature relationship I had ever had with a man. 'We are attracted to each other's minds,' I said.

'What are you blushing for?' she said.

'I'm not blushing,' I said. 'Your eyes are bloodshot.'

'You haven't even been married two years,' she observed.

'Jennifer,' I said, 'I may be married but I'm not in a harem. I can talk to men who aren't eunuchs without being unfaithful.'

'Not easily,' she said. I thought she was being spiteful. It didn't occur to me she might be right.

'He's gay,' I said.

We went to the wine bar everyday and I never once saw him smirk behind my back as we left. I began to think of him as a more intelligent, hairier version of Jennifer.

Then one day, as we sat knee-to-knee discussing Mary at work, who was a secret drinker, he put his hand on my thigh! I stared at it, pretending it wasn't there. 'There must be some mistake,' I thought. He kept his eyes on my face.

'Let's go back to my flat,' he said.

'What for?' I asked.

'For lunch,' he said. 'And a lie-down.'

'I'm married,' I said. 'You know that.' I laughed pleasantly to try and save the situation.

'So?' he said, tightening his grip on my leg.

'I don't lie down with men who aren't my husband.'

'What a dull girl you are,' he said.

'I'm not dull,' I said. 'I'm faithful.'

'You could have fooled me,' he said. I thought I was going to choke on my humiliation. I sidled out from under the horrible pink hand and fled home, where I cried and cried on behalf of my unwanted mind and misunderstood body, until George came in.

I didn't burden him with the disgusting details. I told him I was miserable because I hated my job. 'It's so boring,' I sobbed.

'Then leave,' he said. And I did. I never went back. I rang Mary and told her I was having a nervous breakdown.

'That makes two of us,' she said. I turned to Jennifer.

'I feel like a tart and a fool,' I groaned.

'You sound like a sweet trolley,' she said. She wasn't very sympathetic. She said it was my own silly fault for flirting.

'I didn't flirt,' I said. 'Why would I flirt? I don't want anyone else but George. Not for that.' Not for anything, is what it boiled down to.

'I hope you have learnt your lesson,' she said.

'Shut up,' I replied. But I had, in a way. I had learnt

that relationships all have shapes and you can't trample across their boundaries without doing a lot of damage. Until then our marriage had had about as much shape as a flood. The only line I had recognized was the one George drew at talking.

Suddenly I could see three. One was the hate that was fuelled by our irreconcilable differences, which I had to learn to accept. Another was convention: wives aren't expected to be fascinated by men who aren't their husbands, not every day in a wine bar, and those who look as if they are are asking for trouble. The third was trust.

I could have said George simply didn't care enough to be jealous of my interest in Paul Nolan but I knew that wasn't true. He did just trust me and because he did I couldn't see much point in attempting any more outside liaisons. While I was married to George I had to accept the shape of things. That was the lesson I learnt. I forgot it after a week or so.

CHAPTER SIX

Womb to Rent

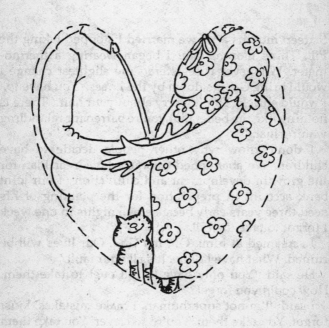

Sixteen months after we married I stopped taking the Pill. Three months later I began wearing a thermometer. Whenever it registered the slightest change I would bring George down by the knees. 'You have to,' I would shriek. 'Don't worry about your hair.' There is nothing like the belief that you're barren for rekindling waning lust.

I don't know why other people decide to have children. We abandoned George's Five Year Plan for the growth, development and cultivation of our joint bank account in preparation for the planting of his seed three years early because two nights in one week I forgot to take the Pill.

I screamed at him: 'Oh, my God. Our lives will be ruined. What have I done. It's all your fault.'

He said: 'You only have to roll over to take them. How could you forget?'

I said: 'I'm not superhuman. I make mistakes. I just forgot. You take them. You're so clever. You take them every night and see what happens.'

It was a sudden thing, my change of heart. One day I was plotting to leave my clothes in a neat pile on Brighton beach and take off for parts unknown, the next I was throwing myself at other women's babies and insisting I wanted one of my very own.

My sister Meg, who was expecting her third child at the time, said, 'You didn't forget. It's not something you forget. You meant not to take them.'

I said, 'There's no need to be bitter.' She was wrong. I didn't want a baby. A baby was the very last thing I wanted for lots of reasons. A baby meant settling down and to me settling down meant rotting away.

I was only twenty-two and I still hadn't done anything. I might have been the life and soul of Henderson and Pit, who were very well-respected solicitors, but this was only a single step up from the Naughtiest Girl In The Class and there were no prospects. I wasn't exactly looking for a career but I was waiting for one to happen. I thought it was just a matter of time before what it was would occur to me. I didn't for a minute think I would go through life unrecognized.

Also, I couldn't help noticing, while I hadn't precisely gone off George, things weren't seething anymore. Of course I cared about him and still found him attractive, but less. You simply can't sustain a passion for a man you see every day in his vest and socks examining his comb. Overexposure has a numbing effect on the glands.

It's a point that's bound to be reached in a marriage of bodies. Some people seize the chance to get out while they can, when there are no children or major joint investments, the relationship has stopped growing and there's someone at the bus stop with better teeth. They say to themselves, 'Why go on when you're going nowhere?' George and I didn't appear to be going anywhere special. Life was more a smile in a bottle than a barrel of laughs and it was my smile that was bottled. I was beginning to feel like a preserve.

Without the passion what was I left with? A man

who was changing shape, whose mind was on hold and for whom I had lost my allure. It was a long time since he'd hung on my every word. The sparkle and life that had attracted him to me now exhausted him. He didn't care much for my extrovert ways. They were all right in a girlfriend but embarrassing in a wife. He was obviously finding me as unfascinating as I was finding him but he didn't need adoration like I did.

After two years of marriage there wasn't much to hold us together: a few records, some wedding presents. There were the vows, of course, but they now held as much sway with me as they did with my mother-in-law. They were words I had mouthed in a ritual I'd gone through in a fit of unwarranted excitement and optimism.

I realized I had never seen a very long future with George, never more than a few months. Growing old together hadn't come into it, anywhere. Two years into our marriage I was quietly looking for a painless way out. I was bored at work and bored at home. I didn't want a baby. I wanted George to make me unhappy enough to leave. But somehow he never did. Then one week I forgot the Pill. Twice.

I began to have morning sickness within hours from fear, which also threw my cycle into chaos. By its thirtieth day I was convinced I was pregnant. I beat my breast in despair. 'You have just committed professional suicide. Your life is over,' I told myself.

George tried to be nice about it. He took out the bank statements and sat hunched over them for several hours. 'It's not really the end of the world,' he finally said.

'It is,' I said. 'I don't want to have a baby and you don't want to have a baby. A baby will ruin everything.' I didn't add I wasn't sure I still wanted him even though the chance was there. I don't know why I didn't. Maybe it isn't as easy as you like to think it is

58

to throw away an investment as large as two years of your life.

George said, 'You're probably panicking. You mightn't be pregnant at all.'

'I am,' I said. 'I am a woman. A woman can tell.'

The very next day it was made abundantly clear by God that I didn't deserve to be pregnant and so should not be. I was elated for exactly five seconds when I discovered I wasn't, then I burst into tears.

'See,' Meg said when I reported this weird reaction. 'You do want to have a baby.'

'I do not,' I said. 'It was relief.'

I rang George at work to tell him the good news. Before I could speak he said, 'I've worked it out. We can put his cot where the chest of drawers is.'

I said, 'We won't have to. I'm not pregnant.'

'Oh,' he said. I thought I heard a whimper. 'So there's no baby?'

'No,' I said flatly. 'Isn't it great?'

'Great,' he said. 'Oh well!' Then he hung up, leaving me alone and barren. That night we celebrated with two bottles of red wine and it was George who asked, 'Would a baby ruin your life?'

'I won't know until I have one.' I said.

We decided at once that we should have one to find out, and to find out what it would look like and whether we were made of the stuff from which greatness might be forged. It was an occasion to remember, so romantic that I palpitate when I think about it. As I gazed at my husband through the rosy glow of Argentine plonk, I saw pounds fall from his waist and face and a glint return to his eye that hadn't embarrassed me for ages.

Deciding to have a baby was like getting married all over again. It gave some purpose to a union that had lost its point along the line. I shut my mind to the

59

reservations I'd been storing up. I found a new set of excuses for my behaviour.

'It's better to have babies young,' I said to Jennifer.

'They look funny old,' she agreed.

'I mean I hate typing. I don't want to spend the best years of my life reeking of carbon paper.'

'You might as well reek of second-hand Ribena,' she said.

I pretended not to hear her indulging my hypocrisy. I told myself it was nothing to do with her anyway and I told myself that although I'd been thinking of running away I hadn't actually considered what I was running away from. If it was only boredom, a baby would soon cure it.

With seven years of motherhood behind me, I can now look back and see what a fool I was. I didn't have the first inkling of what having a baby would mean to me, or to George, or to George and me, or even to the poor little thing we forged. All I knew was that I wanted a baby now and I wanted a baby immediately. And what I discovered in the months that rapidly passed was that the more I didn't have one the more desperate my want became.

Something has to ensure the continuation of the species and I suppose this ignorant obsession is part of it. But there was no sense of responsibility in my broodiness. I wanted a baby to give my existence some purpose. No matter how I saw myself at the time, the truth was that I was only working to earn money to save for a house, which we must all along have intended to furnish with children.

If I'd had a career things might have been different. But I couldn't have wanted a career very badly or I would have done more about it. It must have been status I wanted. All that went out the window, anyway, when we began trying to have a baby. Then it was plain to me that if I was anything I was a born mother.

After a few months I began to think I had been tricked by nature. I started to believe nature had endowed me with mothering instincts that would never be used. Jennifer offered me a cat. 'I'll find one that looks like you,' she said.

Meg said, 'You don't know how lucky you are. I just have to say 'breast milk' and I become pregnant.'

I said 'breast milk' but nothing happened. And nothing happened if we pointed the bed south, stopped thinking about it or concentrated really hard. Some people said if you tried too hard you wouldn't conceive and others said if you didn't try hard enough you could miss the single minute in the month when you were fertile. This was the school of thought I followed.

You go a bit mad when you want a baby. George told me I was mad when I insisted he come home in his lunch hour in case the thermometer moved. I said, 'Do you love me or don't you? Do you want this baby or not? If not, just say so. There are plenty of buses I can throw myself under.' He shrugged his shoulders, which I was once again devastated by, and came home.

He almost never spurned my advances. I can remember only two outright refusals. Once he said, 'Not with my mother in the sitting-room, Tessa. I just couldn't.' And another time he said, 'We are in an off-licence, Tessa. Please remove your hand.'

I think he was afflicted by the same terrible fear I was, that we might fail, although I'm sure no one ever said to him, 'Call yourself a man.' People assumed I was deficient. By people I mean George's mother. She said, 'You can take things for it, you know.'

George had actually told his mother we were trying for a baby. Even now I find it hard to believe. 'Why did you?' I yelled at him. 'Why did you? You know what will happen now? My eggs will seize up completely.'

'To keep her happy,' George said. Mrs Wood had

stopped praying for a divorce. For some time she'd been hoping I would become pregnant and die in childbirth. She began to keep an eagle eye on my figure. 'Everything all right?' she would enquire whenever I went to the loo.

The strain began to take its toll on my body and my erratic cycle became more erratic than ever. I took to sleeping with a pregnancy tester by the bed for inspiration. But George said it put him off so I kept it in the kitchen by the coffee jug. It was constantly in action. I took tests all the time in case my ovaries were lying to me.

Then one month the little red ring appeared under the magnifying glass which meant it had finally happened. I could hardly believe it. I called George to come and have a look.

'What is it?' he asked? 'What am I looking for?'

'A little ring,' I said.

'It's a coffee mark,' he said.

'It's our baby,' I cried.

'It's a very funny colour,' he said. But he was as thrilled as I was. Before I could restrain him he had rushed to phone his mother. 'I'm going to be a father,' he announced. 'You are going to be a grandmother.'

'You can borrow my womb if you want to,' I shouted. George still hadn't worked out who the most important woman in his life was supposed to be.

When he finally managed to tear himself away from her congratulations, warnings of health hazards and requests not to work himself too hard, I took him aside and impressed upon him the fact that it was me. I said if he wanted me to bear him a decent style of child he would have to bear this in mind. He looked at me with something that could have been tenderness and said of course he would. 'But you're not going to be sick all the time, are you?' he added.

I was. All the time. It put our lust pretty well back

where it had been before I stopped taking the Pill. But watching my stomach grow changed the nature of our relationship. It hardened its edges and softened its centre like a peppermint cream.

When I was pregnant I looked at George and thought, 'What have I got?' I had a quiet and caring man, a reliable, solid man who watched over the wife who was bearing his child. I thought about what he had: a wife who was changing shape and whose mind was on hold. For the first time in our lives we seemed utterly compatible.

CHAPTER SEVEN

Labour of Love

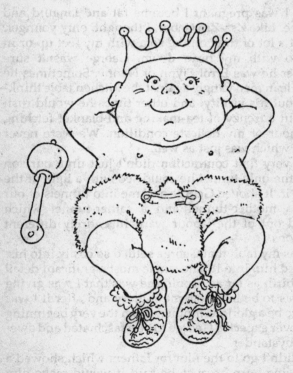

When I was pregnant I became fat and languid and carefree. Like Zsa-Zsa Gabor, I thought, only younger. I spent a lot of time on the sofa with my feet up or in the loo with my head down. George wasn't sure whether he was Errol Flynn or Nanny. Sometimes he would lean menacingly against the kitchen table thinking about his virility, and other times he would rush about in a frenzy of tea-making and blanket-fetching in honour of my delicate condition. We were never closer, which was just as well.

The very first contraction didn't just urge our son down the only tunnel he could see with a light at the end of it. It shoved George and me into tunnels of our own, a mother-tunnel and a father-tunnel which headed out of the labour ward in entirely different directions.

It was my fault that George settled so cosily into his. I pushed him into it. The single most significant detail of the birth as far as I could see was that I was giving it. It was to be my moment of glory and after it I was going to be a glorious mother. From the very beginning I only ever expected George to be a fascinated and awe-struck bystander.

He didn't go to the film for fathers which showed a baby being born because he said it would make him sick. He said he would come to the birth of our baby but he would close his eyes in the bad bits. I said, 'You are very brave.'

I went to the film and I went to all the classes in panting, breathing, relaxing and pushing but they didn't prepare me for the birth because they bore no relation to what I was expecting or what actually took place. They only made me very high-minded.

Since I was going to be a perfect mother I wanted a perfect birth, and a perfect birth was a natural birth. These are births in which the mother can stand the pain, however excruciating. I told myself that I would stand the pain, though I wasn't completely convinced. They said it would only hurt if I panicked but already I could sense a small amount of panic fluttering about the lungs I suspected might refuse to pant on order.

'Will it hurt?' I asked Meg. She had given birth to her third when I was about four months pregnant.

'Depends on what you mean by hurt,' she yawned. She was always yawning.

'Hurt,' I said. 'You know, hurt. Like the time I kicked you in the bosom.'

'Oh,' she said vaguely. 'It's not like that. It's more like a steamroller flattening your bowel.'

'Bowel,' I said.

'Bowel,' she agreed. I don't suppose I was the only woman to waltz into the mother-tunnel with delusions the size of her stomach but 'bowel' meant nothing to me. Nothing at all. Nor did 'steamroller'.

Despite the film, despite Meg, despite the classes, I harboured a vision of childbirth that was beautiful beyond belief. It had dignity in it and no noises apart from soothing murmurs and the final triumphant cry of the baby. They said it would probably be supervised by midwives, and I imagined them to be a couple of ancient but kindly crones who would act according to the age-old traditions of their mothers, their grand-

67

mothers and the Marks and Spencer birth book. George would be there when the baby came out because he had been there when it went in but otherwise it would be private, almost secret. I tried to ignore the prospect of pain.

I went into labour a week early during a dream about giving birth to a cat and I woke up sweating because it was a Persian. It took a while for me to realize I was having pains at regular intervals. When I did I was ecstatic. I couldn't wait to stop being pregnant. I couldn't wait to get it over with. I couldn't wait for the abundant joy.

I savoured the sensation and considered how best to break the news to George, who was sleeping peacefully beside me. 'George,' I bellowed into his ear, 'Wake up. I think it's started.' These are the traditional words a wife says to her husband when she goes into labour.

George said, 'I'm asleep.'

I said, 'Wake up, the baby has started.'

'Started what?' he said. I sighed patiently and rolled off the bed, telling myself it was all I could expect from someone without a womb.

Why I didn't knee him in the back and say, 'It's your baby, you oaf', I'll never know. It was probably the hormones acting on my tunnel. 'Go back to sleep,' I said. 'There's plenty of time.' And he did. Errol Flynn would have. This set him up for life as the one to be protected from anything inconvenient our children ever choose to do – not just being born but waking in the night yelling for Smarties or wanting to wear their shoes on the wrong feet.

I wandered round the flat by myself, humming, getting used to the idea of myself as a mother, looking at myself in the mirror, standing by the window like a lonely young woman in labour, until I decided I was sick of being heroic on my own and woke George again. 'Are you getting up,' I yelled from the doorway, 'or will I give birth in a taxi?'

'I'll just ring Mum,' he said sleepily.

'Are you mad?' I cried in genuine agony. 'This is a happy occasion.'

I wore white to the hospital and I had several white nighties and a white broderie anglaise dressing gown in my bag. This was to honour the purity and innocence of the occasion and its mystical connections with time, space and the special offer at the lingerie shop. George drove at five miles per hour all the way there. 'This isn't a funeral,' I said.

'I don't want to frighten it,' he explained.

Hospitals aren't the friendliest of places at four in the morning. No one was much impressed by the fact that a human being was burrowing its way out of my body. George was shown into a corridor and I was handed over to an ancient crone of about fourteen, who was told to get a move-on with the primitive rites. These were, 'having a bit of a shave down there' and 'emptying the bowel'.

'Just relax,' said the crone.

'I *am* relaxed,' I said. Someone was screaming a few doors along. 'She's having fun,' I observed jovially.

'Out of control,' she said. She was in a hurry to get away because she wanted to get to an all-night party. She told me to have a bath, put on the white apron in the bathroom and go back to bed and wait. She said it would be ages. It always was with the first.

'It's going to be ages,' I said to George.

'Do you want me to wait?' he said. I don't know how he was feeling at the time because I didn't ask him but I think bored could be close to it. He certainly isn't one of those fathers who resents his wife's capacity for child-bearing and longs to be able to do it himself. 'Does it hurt?' he kept asking, and, 'Do you want some crisps? There's a machine outside.'

After about four hours another crone appeared to perform a rite known as 'rupturing the membrane'. She shouted at me for steadying myself by gripping the iron bars on the back of the bed. 'It's not allowed,' she said. 'Just relax.'

'Sorry,' I said.

'Did it hurt?' George asked when he tiptoed back in.

'No,' I lied. I thought if I admitted to myself that it had hurt I would never endure stages two and three.

A strange man peeped around the curtains after a couple more hours and asked if he could 'take a bit of a look'. George said certainly and sidled out. After he had taken his look the man told the second crone that I would need an episotomy. I was no fool. I knew this meant the knife.

'Just relax,' he said as he left. The woman a few doors along had stopped screaming. I thought if I started no one would know it wasn't her.

'All right?' George whispered.

'Fine,' I said. He took my hand and I grabbed it.

'Should you be breathing?' he said.

'If I wasn't breathing I'd be dead,' I assured him.

Just before lunch they wheeled me into the labour ward and strapped my feet into stirrups that were level with everyone's chests. This gave the world a very good view of my bottom. To divert those present from it I asked what the mark was on the ceiling.

'Someone dropped a placenta yesterday,' said a boy who was reading a paper in the corner. 'God, look at this! Pediatrician on murder charge. I studied under him.'

The truly terrible thing about being the central figure in the most celebrated event in the human calendar is that you are naked from the waist down, your legs are spread-eagled in the air, your face is red from exertion, you keep making grunting noises and everyone keeps talking about your bottom.

70

'Push down in your bottom, Mrs Wood,' the two Jamaican midwives told each other when they weren't talking about the awful woman in the private ward. In antenatal classes they had discussed wombs and birth canals and rectums and vaginas in a dispassionate way, as if they had nothing to do with your bottom.

After a few years of pushing a man in a mask said, 'You don't mind a few students, do you?'

'Of course not,' George said, and several hundred people, all of whom were below the age of consent and none of whom had been shown the film, trooped in. I was struck by the looks of incredulity and hysteria on their faces, which were lined up between my legs at the end of the bed looking at my bottom.

'They are looking at my bottom,' I said to George.

'They're watching for the baby,' he murmured soothingly.

'And where's the baby?' I asked.

'Just relax,' said the midwives.

Towards the end of the second stage, when my mind had loosened its hold on my body to escape the steamroller and when people were trying to wrench the mask with the gas and air from my grasp because you can't pant and inhale, I asked myself, how could it be? How could it be that God has allowed men to walk on the moon but he hasn't allowed women to grow babies on their backs in bags with zips? How could it be that we have telephones and radios and stereograms but the navel isn't put to better use? Why must we give birth through the only orifice we know is private and how come thousands of people get to come and watch and tell you to relax?

Back at the entrance to the father-tunnel George was stroking my forehead, repeating everything the midwives said and not being sick once. I was pleased he was there. I would have been very lonely without him. A doctor appeared with some pliers because the

71

midwife said I needed some help. George said, 'I'm going to have to go out for a minute.' Then someone cried, 'Here it is!' and a sea of faces moved towards the end of the bed.

Christopher waited a few minutes before gracing us with his presence, then the steamroller took one last mighty turn around my intestines and he was born. 'You have a son,' the midwife said.

'Don't drop him,' I replied. 'You don't want another mark on the ceiling.'

Everyone laughed nervously. 'He told her about the placenta,' the midwife said to the doctor, nodding her head in the direction of the student.

'Fool,' said the doctor.

They wrapped Christopher in a towel before handing him to me. He looked like a very plain version of the infant Jesus. He didn't seem pleased to see me.

'I don't think he likes it here,' I said to George.

'He'll get used to it,' George replied.

Then they took him away to get him cleaned up for the world at large. George told me he loved me, that he was thrilled with his son, then he kissed me and went away to inform the world at large that he was a father. I was strapped back into stirrups to be stitched up so I could get on with being a mother all in one piece.

The man who did the stitching looked like a shoemaker. I tried not to imagine what it was like from his point of view and I made fascinating conversation about elves to distract him.

'Your son's made a mess of you,' he said. 'Hasn't he?'

'Not yet,' I said grandly. I thought I might as well try and sound grand even if I couldn't look it. When they finally unhitched me I relaxed for the first time in fifteen hours. I didn't feel like a mother. I felt like a used and torn Christmas stocking.

When George came to see me he commented on my

pallor, on the broken veins in my eyes, on the rubber ring I was sitting on and on his exhaustion. He said he'd never been through anything so gruelling.

I told him Christopher was the heaviest baby on the ward. 'Oh,' he said. 'Everyone sends their love.' He asked me where the television licence was, if I wanted anything and when I would be coming home. I asked him who he thought the baby looked like. 'Daffy Duck,' he said. He wasn't so much uninterested as unimpressed. A baby was a baby, even our baby.

Within twenty-four hours it was clear that we now occupied different worlds. His was outside and involved buses and paperclips and decisions affecting the universe. Mine was governed by a small, bald, pink ruler whose main concerns were feeds, changes, baths, weighing and sleep.

I didn't mind because in my world I had a title, which was mother to the king. I was showered with flowers and congratulations and praise and I looked fondly on George as the man who had made it all possible. I hardly noticed the directions our tunnels were taking.

CHAPTER EIGHT

Taking to the Bottle

After two and a half months of motherhood I decided to run away. I packed a bag with Napisan and Farlene and I took off for King's Cross Station, where I hoped to be abducted by a white slave trader. There I discovered I had no money. 'Family life stinks,' I said to the talking clock.

'At the third stroke,' she said, 'it will be six p.m. precisely.'

'There is a feed in the fridge,' I told her.

I wasn't abandoning my baby. I was besotted by my baby. Having the baby was the best part of being a mother. Living with its father was the worst. I was fleeing from George, who, the minute I arrived home from hospital, pretended I wasn't the woman who had gone in but someone out of a DIY catalogue who could build a garage while she made a cake and taught the baby physics. If he had looked carefully he would have seen that those women never have bags under their eyes and they can get into clothes that have waists.

He thought that now I had stopped being pregnant I could settle down to being the perfect wife he'd always wanted. He couldn't see that trying to be a perfect mother might distract me from the task. When it did he thought I wasn't trying.

'I don't understand you,' he said. 'You ought to get a grip on yourself.' But I was too tired to get a grip on anything.

I gave up my plans for being a perfect mother after three weeks when my mother went back to Devon. While she had been there I was reasonably perfect, even though I withdrew my breast when Christopher was two weeks old, or what was left of it because I couldn't stand the pain. His suck could have wrenched Cleopatra's Needle from the Embankment. If I wasn't cracked I was engorged and when I was engorged the health visitor said I had to express by hand.

'It's like getting blood from two enormous stones,' I whimpered to my mother. She recommended the bottle. George's mother didn't.

She said, 'You should persevere for the little boy's sake.' I said the little boy would probably prefer to drink from something that didn't flinch. Mrs Wood rang every day to enquire after the health of her grandson and to see if my mother was still in residence. My mother usually took her calls. She said she didn't know what I had against the woman. My mother is a saint.

While she was there I drifted around in a mist of delight and exhaustion, thrilled by the attention I was getting, amazed at the perfection of the creature I had produced and sleeping whenever it did. I devoted my every waking minute to the tiny little thing, whose fingers curled in a heart-stopping way and whose every sound acted on my system like a cattle prod.

My mother not only took care of the shopping, the cooking and the laundry, she assured me the baby wasn't dying when it gurgled, or deformed when he tried to smile, or backward when he showed no signs of responding to 'Sesame Street'. She saw me through those first weeks when nothing has a proper place any more and she never once poured scorn on my martyr-dom to demand feeding.

George was there, smiling, I think, waiting for her to leave but pleased that the cooking was better than he had ever known and the ironing was immaculate. He went to work every day and he came home at night to an ordered and happy household. Then she left and everything seemed very empty and reduced because the celebration and the spoiling was over and I couldn't get out of my dressing-gown.

The awful weight of Everything I Had To Deal With descended on my undressed shoulders and I discovered I couldn't make decisions. I didn't know whether to try and do the shopping between the nine o'clock feed and the ten-thirty feed, or whether to take the bottle with me and give it to him in the gutter, or whether to do the shopping at all.

Sometimes in the middle of the night I couldn't remember whether I had fed him or changed him and I would go to get another feed but there wouldn't be one there so I would make up a bottle and he wouldn't want it and we would both start to cry and George would say, 'Can't you keep the noise down? I have to go to work in the morning.'

Then all the people I had enjoyed seeing while my mother was there, having been made so welcome, would pop in again to see the baby and stay for hours even though I hadn't sterilized the bottles or changed the nappy bucket or washed up after breakfast. They would talk about their hangovers and their affairs and their jobs, as if they could possibly have interested me. And Mrs Wood kept on ringing. She didn't trust me to manage properly. She knew I couldn't possibly. She feared for the well-being of her son and grandson.

She rang the minute she heard the train door slam on my mother and told George she would be coming over with our supper. She was sure Tessa wouldn't have had time to cook anything. George knew Tessa hadn't. 'That would be lovely,' he said.

'It won't be,' I hissed. 'It's not lovely. We can get fish and chips. Tell her to come next week.'

'Tessa loves tripe,' he said. 'And onions. But you really shouldn't bother. Well, we'll look forward to it. See you in a minute.'

'I'm going to bed,' I said. 'And I'm taking Christopher with me.'

'Don't be ridiculous,' he said. 'Christopher is asleep in his cot and you slept all afternoon. She has a right, you know.'

'What right?' I asked in astonishment. 'She has no right. He's my baby and it's my stomach. If I don't want to put tripe into it, I won't. You eat the tripe and make her happy.'

'Your mother has been here for two weeks,' he said. 'I don't know how you can be so unfair.'

'My mother is different,' I said 'She would never make me eat tripe.'

'You know what I'm talking about,' he said.

'You are talking about your mother coming over here to tell me I'm doing it all wrong,' I said. 'And I'm too tired to listen.' I was genuinely terrified of the Wood influence. I could feel it creeping towards me like an enormous centipede that would crawl into our home and make off with my baby. And my mother wasn't there to protect me.

'She's like Snow White's stepmother,' I said to George. 'And she doesn't just want to be the fairest of them all. She wants to be the best loved, most capable, most important.'

'She is my mother,' he said. 'Kindly remember that.'

'I am,' I said. 'I am remembering.' But I still thought of her as an intruder.

She arrived with the tripe and immediately

demanded to see the baby. Then she picked him up
even though he was asleep.

'He's asleep,' I protested.

'No he's not,' she crooned. And he wasn't any more.
'I'll just wind him,' I said and put out my arms to
take him.

'Good heavens,' she laughed. 'If I don't know how
to wind a baby . . . '

'Let Mum hold him, Tess,' George urged, disguising
his fury with pleasantness. So I did and the boy was
sick in her lap. She went home after a few minutes
because she couldn't get the smell off with soap and
water. George was livid.

'That was a terrible way to behave,' he said. 'You
made her feel unwelcome. She only wanted to help.'

'I didn't make the baby sick,' I said. 'He couldn't help
it.'

'I don't know how you can be so spiteful,' he
snapped. 'It's her first grandchild and your mother's
got dozens. You're being very unfair.'

'Four,' I said. 'My mother has four. And she wouldn't
have come over on our first night alone together in a
month.'

'The reason we haven't been alone together,' he
pointed out angrily, 'is that your blinking mother has
been sleeping on the sofa.'

'Helping me,' I yelled. 'Helping me because you are
too selfish, lazy and inconsiderate to notice I needed
helping.'

'You wanted this baby,' he said. 'You shouldn't have
had him if you weren't capable of raising him! I just
don't understand you.' And he went out to the kitchen
and ate his tripe alone.

I didn't understand myself. I hadn't expected to be
so feeble and I didn't know why I was, apart from the
fact that I never had any time for anything and when
I did I only wanted to sleep. I fed Christopher on

demand because it seemed the only fair thing but I was never sure if what he was demanding was yet another bottle. Finding out seemed to take up hours and hours. I was lost without my mother there doing everything else that had to be done. Orphans manage, I told myself. You have to.

I told George I was sorry I had maltreated his mother, although I wasn't. I only regretted upsetting him. I vowed to pull myself together but I couldn't. I didn't even know which bits wanted pulling. He suffered in silence and if there was only toast for supper he ate it, in silence.

He didn't have much to do with the baby. He would only hold him for seconds at a time as if he was a hand-grenade. He wouldn't change a nappy because he said he couldn't. I said I couldn't either before I had to and George said well he didn't have to. I said but what would happen if you did have to and he said when would that be? I said when I keel over from exhaustion, which caused him to tut noisily. We both knew that if I keeled over he would be round to his mother's as fast as his weedy little legs could carry him. It was the thought of having Christopher raised by Mrs Wood that kept me going.

81

As the weeks passed I did become more organized and less frightened of taking Christopher out with me if I needed something at the shops. People stopped calling in because I was so crabby and I managed to fit in all the work that had to be done: the cleaning, the cooking, the ironing, the shopping, the washing, the feeding, the bathing, the changing and the soothing and the night duties – without any help at all from George. And I managed to have a hot meal waiting for him when he came home.

Then one day I saw this very old woman pushing a pram full of rubbish through the streets wearing an old coat, with her head craned before her like a demented goose, rushing south or somewhere with wild eyes and a lolloping gait. It was me. I scurried home terrified of being recognized, flung off my coat, hurled the baby into his cot and looked at myself in the mirror.

Not only was I a very old lady with deep circles under her eyes, stringy hair and a poor complexion, I was still fat. Instead of looking like an indulged Zsa-Zsa Gabor, I looked like Les Dawson.

'You should see me,' I wailed to Meg. 'I'll never be young again.' Meg, who is a fine specimen of an older sister, said to me – despite her baby, and despite her two other children and her husband Dave, who can be difficult – 'Come and stay for a few days. You need a change of air.' And I went because I have always been selfish.

George couldn't understand why I was going. He said things were just settling down nicely. He swore it would be bad for the baby. 'And what about me?' he said. 'What will I do while you're away?'

'Manage,' I said. 'You only have yourself to look after and I'll only be gone five days.'

The train was wonderful. It didn't need hoovering or dusting or sterilizing and I had everything I needed at my feet, including a baby who slept almost all the way. Meg's was even better. There is genuine order in Meg's house. She runs it like a bus station, although everything happens more or less on time. 'It's the only way I can do it,' she said. Even her baby understood the routine and stuck to it.

After the first day Christopher stuck to it and seemed delighted with six good meals a day instead of twenty. I relaxed and laughed my head off for the first time in months when Meg fell over in the supermarket. When the time came to go I felt prepared to tackle family life, however hideous it turned out to be.

I went home on a Saturday and George met me at the station. We kissed each other with something a bit like pleasure and I decided the coyness in his manner was due to the effort he had put into organizing a welcome home for me. I prepared to be appreciative and tried to remember grateful words for flowers and cleanliness.

I needn't have bothered. There was washing up in the sink that went back five days to the first burnt omelette. There were newspapers and clothes scattered around the bedroom and the sitting-room and the tumble-dryer still had clothes in it from the day I left with mould on them.

'How could you?' was all I said. And all he did was shrug helplessly.

I packed another bag, kissed the baby in his carry-cot and left. I tried not to think about the dear, trusting little face of my son in the mess of his home. I knew George wouldn't let the rats get him, whatever else he might do.

There isn't much a runaway wife without any money can do at King's Cross Station short of curse or offer her body to the first goodlooking stranger. But there wasn't a goodlooking stranger in his right mind who would have looked at my body that day.

I rummaged through my bag looking for stray coins or a lucky £50 note but found only the Napisan and the Farlene. 'He will have nothing for breakfast,' I told myself. 'I will have to go home.' I walked. It took three hours.

On the way I thought about George and the baby and me and George and I began to feel sorry for him. I thought, 'He is feeling rejected.' Fathers can. I read it somewhere. Then I thought, 'If he is trying to punish me with all that washing up he can think again.'

I opened the door to a deathly hush. 'My God,' I thought. 'He has killed himself and the baby.' But he hadn't. He was sitting on the sofa with his son on his lap and they were gazing with fascination into each other's eyes.

'He's a goodlooking boy,' George said.

'I know,' I replied. Then we put him to bed and did the washing up. Together.

CHAPTER NINE

A House Divided

The best way to survive the first year of motherhood is to find another mother whose baby is as weird as yours but not as clever. The best way to survive being married to a mother who is pretending she isn't one is to take to the bottle. That's what George and I found. They mightn't be ideal solutions but they worked for us, by which I mean no one murdered anyone.

By the time Christopher was eight months old I was spending large parts of every day asking complete strangers intimate questions about cat food. Why I did this was a mystery to George. He said he couldn't understand why I was making life so hard for myself. 'Why are you making life so hard for yourself?' he said.

'It's not hard,' I said as I watched the ironing mountain grow where I had hidden it in the airing cupboard. 'I like it.' I didn't just like it. I was addicted to it. I had formed an obsessive attachment to the telephone because it connected me to adult voices that spoke directly to me, unlike the voices on the telly.

Having discovered the joys of a routine at Meg's, Christopher and I had reached a very satisfactory arrangement whereby he thrived and I dealt with the bare essentials, none of which turned out to have any conversation at all. I became a dab hand at getting everything done and keeping everyone happy, but even so I still crashed full pelt into the four homely walls that confine the blooming wife and mother.

I didn't tell George because I was indulging my new passion called Coping Alone. This was part of the Newfound Strength that came from enduring so many aching hours of loneliness. I had decided I couldn't rely on George to see me through the identity crisis that motherhood had forced upon me because, basically I had decided, George was an emotional void. I intended to see it through on my own. This wasn't a smart move.

Motherhood is more like quicksand than quicksand and the only way to conquer it is by joining hands with a long line of people, one of whom is attached to a rock on a bank. I looked at the nearest available people and spurned them all. There was George the emotional cripple, Jennifer, who was newly married to Peter but avoiding babies as if they were bucolic rats, Mrs Wood, whom I regarded as a bucolic rat and Other Mothers, whose friend I could have been but didn't want to become because I feared contamination. I thought if I became their friend they might mistake me for one of them.

I had never seen myself as one of them, not even in my most serene expectations of what a baby would mean to me. I saw myself as a human being who happened to be devoting her life to raising a child. The last thing I wanted was to be sucked into the stifling world I saw at the clinic.

'Got any teeth, has he?'

'Twelve, and he's only a month.'

'Mine's only got eight but he's already sitting up at six weeks.'

'This one's not going to sit up. He wants to walk.'

'Mine doesn't want to walk. He's only sitting up so he can read.'

'Read? Mine can already sing "Hark the Herald Angels Sing".' If I involved myself in that, I thought, I would lose all touch with life beyond. I still wanted to be regarded as part of the mainstream and this was the impression I strove to make on Jennifer, who rang regularly to check my progress. She asked how I was as if she expected to be told any minute of a major catastrophe with the bath water or the play pen.

'I'm fine,' I would say. 'Just been plucking my eyebrows.' I tried not to let Christopher intrude on our friendship or to let it appear that I was so consumed by my interest in him I could think of nothing else.

'Done the nappies?' she would ask, politely.

'They don't take all day,' I would say. Nothing actually took all day. One small, hardly mobile baby, who slept sixteen hours in every twenty-four didn't take up a great deal of time. He just glued me to the flat, where I did nothing. When he was awake I put him on a rug in the sitting-room and gave him some toys and we watched each other doing nothing while the telly blazed away in the corner.

We went for a walk every morning on the common and we went to the shops and occasionally to the clinic but when we weren't doing that we were in because I had no one to visit. And when we were in, after I had done as little housework as I could manage and after I'd fed him and played with him for a bit, we did nothing.

When George came home I would say, 'What did you do today?'

'Oh, the usual,' he would say. 'What about you?'

'The usual,' I would reply. He would creep into Christopher's room and give him a kiss without waking him. Then he would take his shoes off, sit in front of the television and wait for supper. Over his supper he would say, 'How's he been?' I would say, 'Fine.' And if he had grown a tooth, rolled over,

88

chewed on a carrot or uttered a novel sound I might mention it or I might not. It depended on how well I was coping.

Part of coping alone was the rule of silence. I had vowed I wouldn't complain but if I took away the complaints there wasn't much colour to what I had to say. And Christopher's achievements were becoming matters of interest to only Christopher and me. If George found my silence odd he didn't say anything. It seemed to me he quite liked it, that it was what he had wanted all along and that he was under the impression I had matured with motherhood into a log like him.

I said to myself, if this is what my life is to be then this is how it will be. I will be a mother-log, George will be a father-log and Christopher will become a boy-log, and none of us need ever speak to each other unless it is urgent.

The only urgent thing I had to tell George was that I was suicidal but I didn't think he would believe me. And short of throwing away all the aspirins and hiding his razor there wasn't a great deal he could do.

He obviously wasn't going to change nor could he change my life. I had the life I had chosen anyway, the one I had insisted upon. It wasn't his fault that it wasn't what I wanted it to be. The baby was what I wanted him to be but I wasn't. I was repulsive as a slug, and I was bored listening to myself think. In order not to think I kept the television on all day and when Christopher woke up I told him what he had missed.

'Guess what was through the round window today?' I would say if he'd missed Playschool and I would build him a blue tower of bricks next to the red tower, which entranced him as much as it would have entranced Jennifer.

Another woman might have made more of the chores

that needed doing. She might have done the ironing as soon as the washing came out of the dryer, she could have changed the bed more often, cooked more delicacies, kept the flat cleaner, thrown herself more fully into the Mouli. But I didn't. I couldn't.

Another woman might have strapped the baby to her bosom and headed out to art galleries or museums or the countryside. But who is this other woman? And is she mad? I couldn't do any of the things I'd never done before I had the baby because their appeal didn't change with the condition of my womb.

'You can't take to housework just because you've had a baby, can you?' I said to Christopher.

'Urgnoy,' he said.

George's complacency astonished me. I no longer believed he had ever felt rejected. He had only ever wanted to get out of the washing-up and now that he no longer had to share household chores he was in seventh heaven. This improvement was the only impact the baby had made on his life. Otherwise he was carrying on as he always had.

He got up, drank tea, ate toast, got the 8.15 bus, stayed at work all day chatting, laughing, eating, drinking, being important, feeling free, then caught the 5.15 bus home, kissed me, kissed the baby, took off his shoes, watched the news, had supper, asked me why the baby was crying, turned the telly up, looked at his bills, had a shower and went to bed. This to him was being a father.

Of course he doted on his son but he confined his doting to cooing noises over the cot, a short cuddle in the morning, weekend walks with the boy falling off his shoulders, exuberant bursts of affection when he threw him in the air because he was going to be a great little footballer, then irritation when he cried.

'What's he crying for?' he would say. 'He doesn't cry when *you* do it.' Then he would give me a friendly pat and tell me I had the magic touch. Of course I had the magic touch. I spent all day practising, but I was rapidly beginning to feel like the miller's daughter in Rumpelstiltskin, who was locked in a room and ordered to spin straw into gold. My touch had about as much magic as hers. Eventually I cracked and when Jennifer rang to see if I had turned into a nappy, I told her. 'I think I'm going mad.'

'I knew it,' she said. There is no one more maddening than Jennifer for always saying she knew it. 'You need a job.'

'I have a job,' I said. 'He weighs eighteen pounds.'

'I'll get you a job,' she said. 'Something you can do at home when he's asleep.' Jennifer worked for a management consultant organizing other people's lives for them. It was no trouble to her to organize mine. She found me a job with a cat food firm.

George said, 'Doing what?' in amazement.

'Finding out what people feed their cats,' I said.

'You hate cats,' he said.

'I love cats,' I said.

'But what about the baby?'

'I love him, too,' And I found I loved him even more when he wasn't the sole point of my waking up in the morning. I would rush through the chores, dress him, feed him and sit him in his chair while I cleaned the place up. We would go for our walk then I would put him to bed and get on the phone. My fingers itched for the dial even before I had collapsed his push chair.

I would make myself a huge mug of coffee, put my feet up, rest my clipboard on my lap alongside my list of numbers and settle down for a long, long chat. You could tell the ones who only wanted to talk about their flipping cats. I didn't spend much time on them. The ones I loved were the people who had as little to think about as I did.

Of course I sometimes made mistakes and found myself at the wrong end of unsavoury suggestions but I could always hang up on them and usually did. I found some lovely old ladies and one enchanting old man who needed me to explain to him how he could tell if his cake was cooked. And there was Mary Morley. I found Mary Morley in a cat food survey and now she is one of my oldest friends.

I could hear her baby screaming in the background when she answered the phone. 'I'll call back,' I said.

'No, it's all right,' she said. 'She only wants her telephone directory.' She didn't have a cat but she did have Polly, who was not much older than Christopher, and she had a mother who had a cat. She said if I liked she would ring her mother and find out what I needed to know and then she would call me back. I said I could call her mother to save her the trouble but she said her mother was funny.

She rang as I was feeding Christopher and I had to call her back but Polly had just swallowed a bottle top so she rang me back. That's how desperate she was. Then she rang again the next day to tell me her mother's cat had died in the night. I said how awful but she screamed with laughter and I began to suspect there never had been a cat or maybe even a mother. 'She's off her head.' I thought. I agreed to meet her since she only lived a mile away, and we did, on the common, where she turned out to be one of those ravishing women whose babies wear colour-coordinated clothes that fit. I couldn't help liking her anyway. She was as big a mess as I was underneath.

We walked our children in endless circles and we discussed things of such intimacy that we might have known each other for centuries, like cradle-cap and dummies and deformities and head-banging. She knew even less about it than I did although Polly was her second and her baby was about as lazy as Christopher, who was as lazy as George. Talking to her was an unimaginable relief.

When I finally made it back home I was a new woman and I didn't mind a bit that I hadn't made the day's quota of calls. I couldn't wait for George to come in so I could tell him but George didn't come in, not at six o'clock or half past six or even seven. He always came in. He wasn't the sort of husband who stayed out. He never went to the pub unless I dragged him and if he was going to be late he always rang.

At seven I telephoned his office and spoke to Mark Punnet, whom George had told me never went home. I only knew him very slightly in those days but even slightly was enough to find him putrid.

'What, not home? Being a naughty boy, is he?' he said.

'Hang on,' I said. 'I've just remembered. He's gone to his mother's.' I thought if he had gone to his mother's I had no way of finding out. The prospect of notifying her of a rift, if there was going to be a rift, was too chilling for words and there was no point in alerting her to his injury or death until it was certain.

By half past eight I had phoned the police, who couldn't understand the fuss, and all the hospitals between home and his office. 'He's always home by six, you see,' I said to them all.

'I see,' they all said. The police said, 'Call us again in the morning.' At nine o'clock, full of alarm but not in the mood for hearing how it looked from where Jennifer was standing, I rang Mary Morley.

'My husband hasn't come home,' I said casually.

'Mine never does,' she replied. Geoff Morley, who was to become a self-made man, was very busy making himself in those days and to this end he stayed out till all hours, never thinking there was a wife at home who wouldn't have minded if he had delayed the making of his million until his next life-time. His family life ran a very poor second to profit and loss and still does, I think, though both their children are now at boarding school. Geoff named Mary his managing director in charge of home affairs and left her to it, day in, day out.

'Don't you feel neglected?' I asked.

'All the time,' she said. 'I'd give everything for a husband who came home every night.'

'Everything?' I said.

'Every ounce of Badedas I own,' she said. I began to wonder if I appreciated George's worth. It's the sort of maudlin thing you do when you have serious grounds for imagining a fatal accident.

I tried to put myself in Mary's place. She couldn't even look forward to a log rolling in at the end of the day. At least a log was company, especially if he gave you a kiss and enquired after your health. We talked for hours while I waited for the corpse to be brought home, about being a wife and being a mother and what a slog it all was and whether it was worth it in the end for ones so young and beautiful as we were.

Finally she said, 'I don't know. I've got Polly and Ben and I love them. I love Geoff but I haven't got him. That's how it goes.' When I rang off I went and told Christopher that I would try to be a good mother and father to him.

George finally came home at three o'clock, just after I had made a bargain with God. If He spared George, I vowed, I would value him more. He was very drunk and twenty pounds poorer because he had been playing poker with some fellows he used to know from his church youth group.

'You're up,' he said dopily.

'Waiting for the police,' I said.

'Why? What's happened?' he asked.

'My husband didn't come home,' I said. 'I thought he was dead.'

'Sorry,' he said. 'I tried to let you know but I couldn't get '`rough.'

'Let me know what?' I enquired.

'That I love you,' he said. I was too tired to brandish a rolling pin or any other weapon nagging wives are supposed to resort to when they are abandoned by their husbands for booze, gambling and other assorted pleasures. I was even too tired to cry with fury that he had been the one who could stay out on a whim.

'Do you love me?' he asked as he sprawled on the bed.

'Why?' I said.

'I need to know, Tess, I really do need to know.'

'Yes, I do,' I said.

'Good,' he hiccoughed and went to sleep.

After that I stopped coping alone. I didn't need to cope alone once I found Mary Morley, who was worse off than me. She couldn't even see her husband, let alone whether he was attached to a rock on a bank, and George was on the bank, I decided. Even if he was only waving.

CHAPTER TEN

Falling Down on the Job

I progressed naturally from cat food to being a perfect hostess. It was a major development in my life and in our marriage. Not only did it signal the onset of middle age, it taught me to see myself as others saw me and to see George as others saw him. It was awful.

When we were the throbbing centre of a vibrant and glittering social circle we found ourselves married to people who, frankly, failed to come up to scratch. George thought he had married beneath him. I thought I had married a fool. That's what happens when you invite guests into your home. But it began with the cooking.

When the cat food company went bust I found myself with time and energy on my hands and a year's supply of fortified rabbits' livers in lieu of payment. George said, 'Liver will not pay the phone bill.'

I said, 'It must do something.' But it never did. It languished in the broom cupboard until we moved. I, on the other hand looked about for something to do and rapidly became transfixed by Mary Morley looking wonderful behind a hostess trolley. I set my heart on the praise she earned for her performance there.

She had become a perfect hostess in order to see more of her husband. Entertaining his clients with style, taste and skill was one way of luring him home. We were often invited to make up the round twenty at the sit-down dinners she would prepare herself while her mother, who existed after all, took care of Polly and Ben.

The impression this had on me was profound. I stopped resenting cooking and found I actually enjoyed it. I spent days poring over recipes for curried sweetbreads and spinach *boulangere*, always with an eye out for clever things to do with fortified rabbits' livers.

I experimented on George which wasn't easy since he regarded mushrooms as an adventure, but he less and less went to bed hungry and eventually I felt up to going public. I suggested that we give an intimate dinner party with candles and proper napkins for a few close friends where the conversation would bubble like fine champagne, or anyway a medium-priced sparkling white from Sainsburys.

He said, 'What do you mean, dinner party? We've only got five forks.'

I said, 'I know we've only got five forks but I will spend the family allowance on three more.'

He said, 'They won't match. And three forks don't make a dinner party.' I hit him.

I told him it was about time we offered something a bit more exotic than spaghetti and kitchen towel, which had been the extent of our hospitality before we had Christopher. After we had Christopher our social life trailed away and its tiny trickle lead directly from our flat out because I insisted on leaving it whenever George felt up to company.

'If you mean what I think you mean,' George said of my scheme, 'we can't because we don't have a dining-room. You can't give a dinner party in a very small kitchen.'

'I'll make a dining-room,' I said, full of invention now that I could cook. 'At one end of the sitting-room.'

'Which end?' he asked. 'On top of the sofa or under the record player?'

'Are you trying to ruin my life?' I enquired.

'Oh, do it then,' he said. He can be gracious to a fault.

I bought the table and six chairs from a junk shop for £18. I told George they were antiques and a sound investment. He said they looked like bits of junk, which they did until I put a pretty cloth over the table and people sat on the chairs. I squashed the lot into the sitting-room, which suddenly looked like the junk shop and I said, 'There. Now who can we ask with the Morleys?'

Our first dinner party set the pattern for many that were to follow over the next year, while the mania lasted. I asked more people than we could fit around the table and I spent too much on the food. We didn't notice until I began to lay the places that, while I had bought three more forks, I had only bought six chairs. George had to rush across the hall to Mr Ferris, who lent us his rocking-chair and kitchen stool which stuck on the corners in front of the new cutlery that didn't match.

'It looks ridiculous,' George said as the doorbell went, and this was the position he adopted for the rest of the evening. We were both aghast at the staggering behaviour of the other and at the absurd manners produced on our first formal occasion at home.

'Your accent changed,' I said to George in amazement, among the debris later. 'You said 'faaaabulous' six times. Any why didn't you say what you thought about dogs?'

'I didn't want an argument,' he said sulkily.

'You sounded stupid,' I said.

'You sounded pretentious,' he said. 'You have never read *War and Peace*.'

'I have,' I said. 'In Smiths on Tuesday. Not all of it. But I never said I'd read all of it.'

When you ask people into your home what you offer for inspection is what you think you are. George and I hated what the other wanted to be. George thought he was a chap who observed the niceties of the very best circles and I saw myself as the centre of a small, witty, mildly unconventional set of intellectuals who gathered with amusement off a South London high street. George thought my manners stank. I wondered how he dared to parade his low IQ in public. He thought I made him look common. I thought he made me look moronic by association.

Not that anyone was frantically clever at our first dinner party. There were the Morleys, who came late and caused the meat to shrivel pathetically; the Ramsbottoms, who emerged out of George's past to rediscover his strangulated vowels, and Jeremy Burton, the managing clerk from Henderson and Pit who brought his girlfriend Gay. She spilt her wine all over my pretty cloth. 'Don't worry about the table,' Jeremy said to console her. 'It looks like an old one.'

'The insurance will cover it,' George said, and had to leave the room.

I don't know whether it was a success. I was too busy trying to serve food in equal portions to think of anything fascinating to say. I gave Deirdre Ramsbottom so much crab soup that she was almost sick and I left only a spoonful in the pot for me, which I had to stir and sip for ten minutes while Deirdre forced all hers down.

George spoke a great deal to Jimmy Ramsbottom about their very minor public school days when they learnt the airs and graces Mrs Wood had paid for. I thought they sounded lunatic and so did Jeremy and

Gay, who were both mature students and flirting with the Communist Party.

Geoff Morley flaunted his money in a way they found offensive and whenever anyone asked what George thought he simpered and said, 'I try not to think about it.' I laughed shrilly in order to appear unmarried and said what I thought as often as I could just to be polite.

The evening didn't plummet to any serious depths of spite but by the time it was over we knew where we stood. In public we stood as far away from each other as we could possibly get.

Once you start giving dinner parties and your guests start inviting you back your life becomes transformed. You can find circles outside circles outside circles, all of which you may be invited to whirl in. I accepted as many invitations as we could afford and rapidly found myself some distance from the starting point. Certainly everyone was quite a bit older.

Of course we still had friends who took holidays in Turkey and spent their money on underwear but their lives were running at a tangent to ours. They knew nothing about insurance or reject china.

Within three months we had built up a network of friends who saw each other regularly and among whom I saw myself as a bright young thing and very clever for a mother. George went along with our socializing in a comatose sort of way, falling into a middle-aged trance with his first gin and tonic. Everyone thought he was a nice old thing, although he was only twenty-seven, but thick. I could tell they thought he was thick.

'Why don't you say anything when we're out?' I asked him repeatedly. I knew he often had perfectly good thoughts and I was used to him keeping them to himself but no one else was.

'I don't want to,' he said. 'You do enough performing

for both of us.' It was true. I did see dinner parties as performances. They were the focal point of my existence. They determined when I washed my hair, when I shopped, what I bought, which days I read the papers, whether I scanned the financial pages, the arts pages or the small ads and they gave me a reason for polishing nifty little anecdotes. An evening was a complete success if I dominated the table for courses at a time.

George found this gross. 'You don't need to be quite so loud,' he would say in the car on the way home if he was feeling benign. Other times he would snarl, 'God, you're embarrassing.' He used to instruct me in etiquette: 'Don't insult our hosts by fighting with another guest,' and so on. He didn't believe me when I told him I knew what I was doing. He didn't believe me when I told him he was a bore. Neither of us believed in the view the other had.

I certainly didn't consider myself loud. As a sophisticated cordon-bleu mother I mostly confined my showing off to sparring with the man on my right or left or occasionally crossing the table to demonstrate the breadth of my knowledge and the depth of my reading, which I acquired from reviews and editorials. I only went for the whole table if I was very sure of myself, the table not too big and I'd had enough to drink. I hardly ever spoke to the women because women were daytime in my book. I might see them for lunch or tea and talk to them on the phone to arrange another dinner party but I didn't have anything to say to them at night. I loved the dinner parties for the flirting, the praise, the laughter, the cooking, the praise, the company, the dressing-up, the excitement, the drink and the praise. I scarcely gave George's lack of enthusiasm a second thought.

I loved them until the night I gave a dinner for twelve and drank too much in the company of a man who knew more about the Common Market than I did, while the main course burnt in the oven.

It was *Boeuf* something and the man was very good-looking. I was thrilled to have him in my house although I hardly knew him. His wife was a friend of Deirdre Ramsbottom and she was the one who had agreed to come. Because he was so good-looking I stood by his elbow while George served drinks before dinner and when the conversation turned to the Common Market I began with a flourish, not caring at all that I knew as much about it as I knew about pre-war Chad. It was the sort of flourish that allowed no going back.

'Of course it's a fraud,' I declared, taking another drink and telling myself that *Boeuf* could stay forever in the oven without spoiling.

'Why?' he enquired, for one fantastic minute mistaking me for a woman of learning and well-based opinion. He discovered almost immediately that I wasn't because I couldn't say why and he turned to George who looked glassy-eyed and said he wasn't especially interested.

'People are getting hungry,' he said to me, quietly.

'No they're not,' I said. 'Pour more drinks.' I wanted to salvage my standing before sitting.

I banged on about subsidies and farmers and mountains and anything else I could think of that showed I read the papers and was a force to be reckoned with, but it was too late. The man from Brussels had written me off. I resented being written off in my own home even if smoke was starting to belch from the oven and George was pulling at my elbow.

'You are a bore,' I declared loudly. 'I don't care how handsome you think you are.' Someone hiccoughed nervously, me I think, and I wondered how much I had had to drink. George called everyone to the table.

There was nothing wrong with the salmon mousse

which I had made earlier. Everyone ate it very quickly, before I had time to scrape the *Boeuf* out of the pot and on to the plates. George came into the kitchen. 'We can't eat that,' he said. So I didn't serve it. I gave everyone a charred potato in its jacket and rapidly produced the pudding. There wasn't a guest left in the house by half past ten. They just made their excuses and left.

I regretted everything the minute I hit the pillow and the ceiling began to revolve maliciously. 'I'm sorry,' I said to George.

'I'm not,' he said. We stopped whirling after that. I decided I didn't like the way people saw us and that we were both misunderstood. The hole in my life hardly mattered because it was rapidly filled by a baby. Nine months to the day after I ate that charred potato I had Katy.

CHAPTER ELEVEN

Christmas Spirit

Neither George nor I showed any neurotic symptoms after the birth of our second child. We enjoyed it from its beginning to its end, which was rendered painless by every unnatural device I could lay my hands on. But I've often thought since that the insanity of the Christmas a couple of months later was a delayed reaction.

That was the year we tried to be in three places at once and I discovered there was only one good reason for not hitting your mother-in-law. It was also the year I discovered that married couples should avoid Advent. But I discovered it too late. It is a lesson I will teach my children. If you must marry, I will tell them, avoid Advent. Advent is the season for councils of war when families-in-law abandon peaceful negotiations and bring on the heavy artillery. The issue is always the same: whose house should dispense the Christmas joy.

The choice is usually clear. Offend one set of parents for life or never talk to the others again. Everything you ever suspected about your in-laws turns out be true at Christmas time. The star of Bethlehem shines on the world between your family and his.

For the first five years of our marriage George and

108

I did the right thing by his parents and tackled a festive goose with them over a subdued and unnaturally joyless lunch. I did it for George and George did it for them. He said he couldn't let them have Christmas on their own. He said he owed it to them. They had raised him, after all. I told him that he owed it to himself to enjoy Christmas for once as my family did but he didn't like to. George honoured his mother and his father.

Those Christmas days were only made bearable by the presents George gave me in the morning and the prospect of Boxing Day when we would leap into the Morris Minor and head for Devon, a mere ten hours away, if we hurried.

But the year we had Katy was also the first year when Christmas meant anything to Christopher and I wanted him to have a normal first impression. I wanted him to see that it was a time for fun. I didn't want him stuck in a chair piled high with cushions for hours on end with an overstarched napkin tearing at his neck while Mrs Wood at the head of the table urged him to sit up straight, have nice manners, eat up the stuffing and not play with his pudding. I wanted him to see that talking was allowed and laughing and singing and eating sweets before lunch because everyone else was too busy enjoying themselves to notice. I wanted him to be with his cousins and make a lot of noise and demonstrate to his maternal grandparents that their daughter was producing a child of substance. I wanted him to sense the goodwill towards men which flowed in my parents' house.

The difference between Christmas with the Woods and Christmas with my parents was the difference between George's and my personal histories. If I was appalled by his, he was astonished by mine. He never knew family life could be so noisy and frivolous. He thought our jokes were pathetic. They are but they're better than no jokes at all and because they've been the same for years they provide a warm and comforting continuity that reassures the bit in me that can't grow up.

It's not just the difference between being an only child and one of three. It's different parents. Mine like each other. They like a good laugh and they laugh easily and often. I'm not sure I've ever heard George's mother laugh. She probably did once but I wasn't there for it. The woman is a stickler for refinement and things you laugh at are hardly ever tasteful. How she came to have a baby I'll never know. George is a success story for nature in its battle with nurture, though nurture still weighs heavily with him. I had to steel myself to say, 'I want to go home for Christmas this year,' because I knew how awkwardly it would place him.

What I hadn't taken into account, however, was the effect of his baby daughter upon him. By the first week in Advent, when she was six weeks old, he was so besotted by her he was prepared to do anything for her mother, even tackle his own.

'Good idea,' he said. We agreed to drive down to Devon on Christmas Eve and stay for a week. I was delighted we had settled it so easily.

George broke the news over his mother's head at tea the following Sunday, the second in Advent. I wasn't in the room so I didn't hear what he said but I saw neighbours cringing behind their curtains at the effect. She marched into the sitting-room where I was giving Katy her rose-hip syrup and her husband was snoring quietly in his chair by the smouldering gas logs.

'Harry,' she shrieked. 'We'll have to cancel our plans. They're not coming here for Christmas.'

'Wha . . ?' said Harry.

110

'Tessa is taking the children to Devon. Leaving us on our own.'

'Oh,' he said, groping for a suitable opinion. 'Well, then.'

'After twenty-seven years,' she said, 'it has come to this. I don't know how you could be so callous.'

'Sorry,' said her husband.

'Twenty-eight,' said George. 'I'm twenty-eight.'

'I don't know what's callous about it,' I said with postnatal fury rising in my rib-cage. 'It's my turn.'

'What have turns got to do with it,' she cried. 'When your mother has three children and we only have George?'

'You should have had more,' I snapped. 'Your family planning's got nothing to do with me.'

'Tessa,' George gasped.

I struggled to my feet, which were somehow encased in my Mothercare baby-bag, and with the rose-hip syrup still plugged into the baby's mouth I tried to confront Mrs Wood with dignity. She was pretending to collapse from shock and grief.

'Did you hear that, Harry?' she gurgled. 'I have never been spoken to like that. To think our son could have married such a girl. She is driving him away from us.' For a dying woman she had an awful lot to say.

'Oh, shut up,' I said.

'Tessa,' George gasped again. 'Apologize to my mother. You can't talk to her like that.'

'It's about time somebody did,' I said. But my anger had already gone. I told her I was sorry but I said I was still taking the children to Devon because I wanted my family to see Katy.

Christopher took this opportunity to break into heart-rending sobs. He had been playing quite happily among the flower pots lined up on the window

111

ledge but suddenly he was assailed by the tension. He wiped compost all over his face as he wept.

Mrs Wood leapt to her feet. 'Oh, my God,' she screamed. 'What's he done? You must be out of your mind dragging him away from his home at Christmas time.'

I thought I might slap her. I moved towards her, frantic to slap her and would have had it not been for the bottle in one hand and the baby in the other. Christopher, sensing the itch in my palm, wailed, 'No, Mummy, no,' and in a flash I understood that if I hit her I would be hitting his grandmother. This is why you must always control yourself – for your children.

George picked up the sobbing child and said, 'Be quiet, Christopher. There's nothing to cry about.'

'Come to Granma,' cooed Mrs Wood. But he wouldn't. He buried his face in his father's neck and aimed a karate kick at her head.

Mr Wood said, 'I don't know why everyone is upset. Surely Tessa isn't thinking of going away for the whole of Christmas.'

'Until New Year's Eve,' I said hopefully.

'Oh,' he said. 'She is. Can't you just buzz off on Boxing Day or something?'

'No,' I said. 'It's Christmas I want to spend with them. I haven't for years.'

'She's right, you know, Mum,' George said. 'It's only fair.'

'Fair?' she cried. 'Did you think about what was fair to me?' Mrs Wood is not a stupid woman. Her cleverness is to ignore the other side of the coin. I've heard her argue with elderly and infirm customers when they've tried to return faulty garments and her logic would defeat the Archbishop of Canterbury.

'Look,' I said, suddenly overcome by the awfulness of the situation. 'Let's leave it. We'll go home and work it out. I'm sure we can think of something that suits everyone.'

'The only thing that will suit me is what we did last year.' Mrs Woods sniffed. So we went home and when the children were asleep in bed I kicked George because he was the son of his mother.

'You should have put her in her place,' I said.

'I feel sorry for her,' he said. And I did, a bit. As sorry as I felt for the Ugly Sisters when the shoe didn't fit them.

I telephoned my mother to put her in the picture. 'I see,' she said. 'Well, I won't pretend I'm not disappointed. We were looking forward to having the whole family.'

'But what can I do?' I said.

'It's up to you,' she said.

'It's up to you,' I said to George.

'It's not that easy,' he reminded me. We considered as many combinations of Christmas arrangements as we could but there was the inescapable difficulty of two hundred miles between one house and the other.

'I will not eat another goose in your mother's house,' I declared. 'It's not like Christmas. It's like Good Friday.'

'Well I can't let them spend Christmas on their own,' said George. 'I have a duty to them.'

'Don't they have any lonely friends?' I asked. 'There must be people who have something in common with them. If only the Hitlers were still alive.'

'There's Aunty Muriel,' George said. He suggested Aunty Muriel to his mother, Aunty Muriel being her cousin, but she said sourly, 'You know she gets on my nerves.'

Defeat was inevitable. It had been from the beginning. But I fought hard for conditions. I said lunch had to be at our place, that we would feed Mr and Mrs Wood and then we would drive down to Devon and get there just in time to see everyone going to bed after a wonderful family day without us.

My mother said, 'She's being a little unreasonable.'

I said miserably, 'I was looking forward to it.'

My mother said, 'We'll just have to put it back a day.'

'Christmas has never been on the 26th,' I said glumly. But for our family it has been ever since. We postpone every year's Christmas to keep Mrs Wood happy.

That year, however, she didn't care for the deal. She objected to the idea of us leaving after lunch. 'You can't now,' she said. 'Not now I've organized Muriel. She was your idea and she's only coming to see the children.' So were the dozen or so other very distant relatives she had summoned for Christmas supper to ensnare her son and pay back her daughter-in-law.

'I'm going to kill her,' I said to George.

He said, 'They'll send you to jail. Think of the baby.' He marshalled his reserves, however, and informed her that we would not come to supper but we could drop by for tea on our way out of London. If Muriel was there then, we would see her.

I said it was in the opposite direction to Devon but he said, 'Please, Tessa, don't make things awkward.'

So that's how we spent that Christmas, falling over ourselves to please everyone. The Woods didn't enjoy the lunch because I left the giblets in the turkey and they have never been again. It wasn't just the turkey. It was also the paper hats that Mrs Wood was made to wear even though she wanted her set to last three days.

I still haven't had Christmas Day with my family during this marriage. That Christmas was the thin end of George's mother's wedge. We now even stay for her supper and leave for Devon before dawn next morning.

I have yet to hit her. I now call her Hatty in honour of the chorus girl she told me two Christmases ago she once wanted to be: Hatty Divine. But it hasn't really made life much easier. The rule for family Christmases is that the least deserving person always gets their own way. I think that's how Jesus would have wanted it.

CHAPTER TWELVE

Mental Health Centre

My secret life began when Katy was six months old and I decided I wanted to go out to work. It wasn't the same as coping alone, which, let's face it, had been a *cri de coeur*. It was a matter of common sense. I had to protect me from George and George from himself.

George thought he didn't want me to have a job but I knew that he would prefer it to me not having one because I knew what I would be like if I continued not to have one. I would not only be poorer, I would be crackers. I didn't want a career. I just wanted to work for a few hours each week for money and a small flicker of recognition.

I didn't burden George with this because his frame of mind couldn't have stood it. But I needed to burden someone so I tried it on Jennifer. This was very stupid. Jennifer was no longer the friend she had been. Jennifer had produced three children in the time it had taken me to have Kate. While this would have turned any normal woman into a whimpering wreck it had had precisely the opposite effect on her. She turned into a Mother Ad Nauseum.

'What do you mean, "crackers"?' she asked. 'How can you abandon your baby when she is only six months old?'

'With a smile,' I lied.

Jennifer had actually been pregnant with Rosie when she had lined me up with the cat food company but she hadn't known it and a year after having Rosie she had the twins. This extravagance led her to believe that she knew more about mothering than anyone else in the history of mothering, especially me.

Her philosophy for child-raising, as she spelt it out to me over and over again, always contained a hint of accusation. She believed in a twenty-four hour commitment and she didn't approve of me hankering after something else even though I hankered after so very little.

All I wanted was to get up on a couple of mornings each week, put on make-up and unstained clothes and head off with a purpose, on my own, to a place that would pay me money for my time and energy where no one would call me Mum.

After Jennifer said, 'You probably should never have had children,' I stopped talking to her and started talking to Meg. Meg didn't go out to work herself but she intended to and she didn't object to me wanting to. 'It's just so difficult to arrange,' was the only discouraging thing she said.

It was difficult. It even looked impossible for a while. I had to find a child-minder who wasn't a murderess for one thing, and a job that kept nursery school hours.

It was Christopher starting nursery school that had prompted me to think the whole thing was possible. Surely, I thought, there would be a glut of kindly ladies longing to care for Katy without Christopher.

'If you don't want to, why should anyone else?' George asked drily. This was before I decided he couldn't handle it. I ignored him and I ignored Jennifer and I set out like the Little Red Hen to do it all myself. I did it in my usual fashion. I waited for irresistible opportunities to fall into my lap.

The first fell off the notice board at the nursery school in the way of a small white card from a child-minder claiming years of experience and good references. I studied the handwriting carefully, looking for loops and twists and careless joins that might suggest deviance or cruelty or deafness. Jennifer had warned me of deaf child-minders. She said they left babies in their prams all day and let them cry themselves hoarse even though there were nappy pins sticking into them and they hadn't eaten a thing since breakfast.

I asked Pat, the nursery school teacher, if she could recommend this one. 'Floss McIntyre?' she said. 'Lord, yes. She's looked after lots of ours, even some really awful ones. I'm amazed she's still at it.' Then she hurried away to wrench a child from a puddle of glue.

I didn't tell George or Jennifer or even Meg about Floss McIntyre, not in view of Pat's amazement. I arranged a secret visit and went to be amazed for myself. It turned out to be her age that was amazing. She was on the brink of retiring.

'I don't really want another baby,' she said. 'I was sixty last birthday.' She made it sound biblical. She looked biblical, with her snowy white hair and her saintly face, which had come from years of being serene in the face of adversity. She admired Katy and we talked for a while. She invited me into her kitchen so she could watch Natasha, who was in the garden.

She'd had Natasha since she was a baby three days a week, she said. But now she was off to big school. She still had Phillip, whom she collected each day from Christopher's nursery and she thought she would like someone to keep him company. When they went to big school, she said, she would retire. Well it was her husband. He was going to retire and he didn't want a horde of children about the house. She said she would happily take Christopher.

'You wouldn't want him,' I said. 'he's much worse than Katy.' She laughed.

'They don't worry me,' she said. I looked at her large hands and wondered if she had ever used them for spanking or strangling.

We chatted about children and the nursery school and children's appetites and jobs and the war and why she became a child-minder and how anyone did it these days and some of them were shocking and then she admired Katy again.

'What did you say your job was?' she asked. I explained I didn't have one but that I was looking for something in the mornings. I glanced about her house, at the old pram in the hall and the high-chair by the fridge and thought about the number of children who had been strapped into them for punishment.

'She's a darling,' Floss said. 'I don't know. Maybe I could manage her. But she will be my last one.' My heart sank.

'That's wonderful,' I murmured. 'I'll let you know as soon as I find a job.' And I scuttled out with my baby as fast as I could. You couldn't trust a woman as nice as that, I told myself. I was pleased I hadn't mentioned her to anyone.

She rang that night just as George and I were sitting down to supper. 'I know you were only wanting mornings,' she said, 'but Natasha's mother is leaving her job and I thought it might interest you.' It was a medical clerk's job at the health centre between her place and mine from nine to four on Mondays, Wednesdays and Fridays.

It was too many hours away from the baby. I wasn't interested, not really, not very much, well, not at all, especially. 'Thanks for thinking of me,' I said.

'Who was that?' George asked.

'Someone from the nursery,' I said.

I wandered along to the health centre the next day

just to see what it looked like. And that afternoon I called by the McIntyre's house just as Natasha's mother was collecting. She told me the job was certainly going and I thought the pay wasn't bad.

'It's boring, though,' she said. 'And the woman I work with can be a cow. I wouldn't take it unless I was desperate. I'll suggest you if you like.' I wasn't desperate, was I? I didn't know. How desperate is desperate?

I went for the interview and got the job. Then I told Meg. I said I was desperate. And I said medical clerk was better than dinner lady or cleaner. Of course it wasn't as good as interior designer or brain surgeon but brain surgeons keep very awkward hours.

Meg said, 'What have you got to lose?'

'A husband and two children,' I said.

'Take it,' she urged. So I did. George hit the roof. I told him that Floss was an even better mother than me and she would have Katy three days from nine to four, and Christopher three afternoons after school.

'We know nothing about her,' he said.

'*You* know nothing about her,' I corrected him. I've talked to her for hours. Twice.'

'She's too old,' he said. 'Sixty. It's ridiculous.'

'Your mother is fifty. An old fifty. This woman is a young sixty. You can hardly tell the difference.'

'I don't like it,' he said. I started the very next Monday with him still not liking it. He was hardly talking. I wasn't really liking it any more but I thought it was now or never. I mightn't have another chance.

I left Katy asleep in her pram in Floss's sun-room and I cried all the way to the nursery. Christopher, who had marched into school every day as if he couldn't wait to escape my clutches, decided on the spur of the moment to support his father. The minute I tried to kiss him goodbye he yelled as if I had amputated his head.

'This isn't like you, Christopher,' Pat said as she loosened his knuckles from my thigh.

'I hate you, Pat' he said.

'Never mind,' she murmured soothingly and prised him away just as the NSPCC took their first call of complaint.

I reported for work with all the enthusiasm of a cow checking into an *abattoir*. All I wanted was to go home and do yesterday again. Yesterday I had been the mother of two happy children with a husband who talked to her.

The name of the cow I worked with, who was actually my boss, was Mrs Finch. She was a woman in her middle-fifties who had worked all her life. She was widowed and extremely disappointed. Life hadn't handed her any favours so she wasn't inclined to hand out any to anyone else.

She wasn't remotely interested in my domestic arrangements or in the size and shape of my family. All she wanted was for someone to do the job properly. It wasn't a hard job but she wanted it done properly. Because she wanted it done properly I found it hard to master the details, like opening cupboards and tidying shelves. She said grimly, 'Well, it's your first day.'

I spent a lot of it hearing Katy and Christopher crying and instinctively turning to them only to realize they were someone else's children in the creche or the waiting room who didn't need me.

As I picked up all the drawing pins I had dropped by the store cupboard I wondered what on earth I was doing there when I could have been at home, picking up my own drawing pins, with Katy burbling happily beside me and Christopher falling over in them and getting tetanus. I asked myself where was the stimulation in drawing pins, where was the company, where was the skill in picking them up and whose idea had it been in the first place?

123

Mrs Finch didn't talk much. She introduced me to anyone we came across: a terrible health visitor called Jane, a couple of other young health visitors, a few receptionists, a chiropodist and a cleaner. They all said hello then forgot I was there.

At lunch-time I rang Floss to find out how everyone was and thought I could hear Christopher sobbing in the background. 'Can I hear him crying?' I laughed.

'It's the telly,' she said. Telly? She was plonking them in front of the telly all day. Oh, God. She was going to turn them into vegetables.

'He doesn't watch much television usually,' I trilled, trying to quell the hysteria gnawing at my throat.

'It's only Phillip playing with the controls. Phillip!' she yelled.

'How has Katy been?' I asked to drive out the image of an electrical fire and flames so fierce no one could fight their way through.

'She's a dear little thing,' said Floss. 'I've put some of my cream on her nappy rash.'

'What nappy rash?' I whispered. She'd had no nappy rash that morning. Had she been scalded or burnt with cigarettes?

'She's teething, isn't she?' said Floss. 'Still, she won't die of it.' I hung up with a lump entrenched in my throat. If she died of her teething nappy rash, I thought, I wouldn't be there to say goodbye. I would be too busy counting staples. And what was the child-minder doing anyway, telling me my daughter was teething before I told her?

I survived the afternoon by concentrating on the demands of the job, which Mrs Finch said were cleanliness, courtesy, neatness, organization, discretion and reliability. She actually wanted a Girl Guide, not a demented mother who hankered after glamour and her children.

'We must respect the patients' privacy,' Mrs Finch

said. 'You'll see and hear a lot that you must simply put out of your mind.'

I longed to ask her if she meant terrible diseases or adulterers but you could almost touch Mrs Finch's high moral tone. She was no fun. At the end of the day, however, she said she hoped I hadn't found it too exhausting and she looked forward to seeing me on Wednesday.

I rushed to the child-minders, preparing myself on the way for carnage and misery. Floss opened the door with Katy on her hip, who beamed at me and held out her arms to prove that she hadn't forgotten who her mother was.

'Where's Christopher?' I asked, looking in the corners for a small crumpled heap.

'In the garden with Phillip,' she said. 'Killing worms, I think.'

By the time George came home that night I had fed and bathed the children and prepared our supper. I had been so pleased to see Katy and Christopher that I hadn't shouted at them once, even though Christopher whined nonstop from the moment we walked through the door. I found I had the patience of Job, if it was Job who had patience, the patience of my job even though it was only tidying up and being agreeable. Guilt-induced patience is the most enduring kind.

George, startled by my efficiency, was moved to ask, 'How was your day?'

'Wonderful,' I fibbed because it was my secret life. 'The best I've had in years.'

'Oh, good,' he said. And that was that.

I am still a medical clerk and Floss has become the person in the world I most rely on. She is the staunchest ally in my life beyond George.

Because it began as a secret, my job is regarded as my problem and any inconveniences it causes are up to me to solve. It is not supposed to intrude on George's well-being because it's something I brought upon myself. It gave me the life of my own I wanted and I think I'm grateful.

CHAPTER THIRTEEN

Sex After Marriage

Being unfaithful has hardly anything to do with sex. Husbands and wives sneak away from their marriages to have affairs because they are lonely, bored, unloved, depressed, taken for granted, insecure, ageing or flattered. I ought to know. I've never had one.

The reason I've been so relentlessly faithful to George also has nothing to do with sex. It is fear: fear of losing what I know I can live with and fear of retaliation. This took some working out. My life has not been without Temptation.

I'm not talking about Paul Nolan. His bed was as tempting as the rack. I'm talking about the real thing.

I was twenty-seven, married seven years, with two small children aged three and one, a part-time job that made me feel free and a husband whose idea of foreplay was to sigh noisily until I put out the light, no matter how good my book was. Nothing wrong with that. All married couples have codes. Meg's husband makes turkey noises at her.

We still had our steamy moments but after seven years they tended to take us by surprise. We were comfortable together. The only thing we ever argued over was who was tireder: me with my job, the children, the housework, the shopping and the laundry to see to – or him, bringing home his heavier pay-packet.

Sex after marriage is a funny business. They say it happens in households across the country twice weekly year in and year out, binding couples together, tearing them apart, sending them to sleep and giving them time to think about the cracks in the plaster on the ceiling. They say it gets better with practice and I suppose it does. But you can't practise passion unless it's how to fake it and faking it does nothing for the ego.

When I was twenty-seven I had a single ego trapped inside a married body and although it didn't show, I think George did too. We had been married too long for ones so young. That must have been it. In me, it showed. This was before we had a mortgage, of course. I spent every penny I earned on clothes, makeup and haircuts and if I was chatting to male patients in the waiting room who were under fifty and not too sick I would pretend I was single.

In the married woman this produces an extraordinary effect. The normally hostile married mouth relaxes into an expression of welcome. The hunched body straightens and hums and the distracted, weary eyes glint and flash. I saw it happen in the glass that blocks off the receptionists' desks.

Pretending you are single, however, means pretending you are available. I only wanted to look available for seconds at a time, just for the reaction. I didn't realize it was habit-forming. But by the night of Mr Ferguson's retirement party, I was hooked.

Although it was only Mr Ferguson's retirement party, I dressed for an orgy. Christopher noticed. 'You look funny,' he said.

George said, 'Hurry up. Don't worry about your make-up.'

Mr Ferguson was the managing director before last

at Mathesons, where George has worked all his life. The party was thrown by his third wife, a ravishing woman half his age who understood the laws of testate.

I didn't immediately see Mrs Ferguson's brother because the giant drawing-room was crowded with everyone Mr Ferguson had ever sucked blood from in the course of his long career and it was very dark. George said, as he steered me towards Mark Punnet's wife, 'We won't stay long, just long enough to be polite.' But he seemed oddly anxious to circulate and before long he left us to dart off and talk about luncheon vouchers with a couple of typists, who seemed to think he was the bee's knees.

I had nothing to say to these typists. I had nothing to say to Mrs Punnet, who looked as if she was made of crushed violets. We talked about fares. Then we talked about packed lunches and she kept referring to me as 'women like you', as if I was some sort of Amazon who could plough through the world undaunted by volcanoes, flash floods or the weekly shop at Safeway.

'I wish I had your energy,' she whispered. I was on the point of denying that I had any to speak of when Mrs Ferguson brought over her brother. He was as ravishing as she was. Everything on him rippled.

'Here she is,' she gushed. 'Here's the woman you wanted to meet.' I beamed at them. 'Andy, this is Mrs Punnet. This is Doreen.' She gazed at me blankly even though we had been introduced only seconds before. 'I'm sorry,' she said to my grinning face.

'Tessa,' Doreen cried in embarrassment. 'This is Tessa Wood.'

Mrs Ferguson glided off to inspect her silver, leaving us with her brother. I couldn't take my eyes off him. He couldn't take his eyes off Doreen, who was wearing something in sorrow and misery.

He had barely opened his mouth to suggest an

assignation when out of nowhere her husband plucked her from our midst and carried her off like a small, dark insect with her spindly legs dangling sadly behind her. 'Come on, dear,' he yelled. 'I'll have to feed you. You can't hog the limelight all night.' And she was off before Andy could utter a word. His eyes, I noticed, followed her all the way to the supper table. My husband had vanished, I also noticed with relief.

'She knew my mother,' he said. I won't deny that this capacity for being fascinated by Mrs Punnet had something to do with my anxiety to interest him. I won't deny that I didn't glow from the waist up when he turned his probing green eyes on me and asked what I did for a living or that my heart didn't ache when he told me he was a professional golfer.

But that wasn't why I spent the whole night with him, went out on to the balcony with him, kept pace with his drinking or told him that apart from Paul Nolan I had been faithful to George for seven years. That wasn't why I admitted that I found other men attractive or why I tried to impart some of the vulnerability that was patently so charming in Mrs Punnet. I only did this because I felt sorry for him. His mother had died, knowing Doreen Punnet. I gave him my phone number at work as a mark of sympathy. There was nothing untoward about it, nothing I wouldn't have told George. But George didn't ask. I didn't see George all night, as a matter of fact.

He sought me out shortly after two and said he thought it was time we left. He found me on the sofa with Mrs Ferguson's brother, whom he nodded to politely. He didn't seem to hear Mrs Ferguson's brother tell me I was the most beautiful woman in the room and if he did he presumably thought it was my nature we were discussing which in a way, it was.

We didn't talk much on the way home. He was far

too tired and I was far too happy. 'Wasn't bad, was it?' George murmured as he closed his eyes.

'Not bad,' I agreed. It was the admiration that made me happy and the undisguised interest in those green, golfing eyes.

Mrs Ferguson's brother rang the very next morning, just as I reached work feeling Georgeless and childless. My head ached appallingly, a single woman's headache, but it hardly touched my joy. He asked me to lunch.

'You know what I think about lunches with men who aren't my husband,' I said.

'But I'm different,' he laughed. 'I know where I stand.' He spoke with such confidence that I couldn't resist him.

I met him for lunch on a Thursday, a day when I would normally have been with my children, absorbing strength from family life and showing them how to get the foul grey ring off a bath. I left them blithely with Floss and I didn't bother telling George. There was nothing to tell him. He didn't like golf.

Over the cold soup, which I will always remember because I choked on it, we gazed into each other's eyes and brushed hands on the crisp white tablecloth. We indulged in perilous talk of other people's infidelity, Mr Ferguson's sexual preferences, George's stability, Doreen Punnet's baleful eyes, the need for seizing the moment and how nice it was that we'd met. His dead mother turned out to be a dull woman.

Floss looked puzzled by my over-enthusiasm when I collected the children and the fumes of wine and garlic in which I was floating but she said nothing. George telephoned to say not to bother about cooking supper for him because he was running late and had had a large lunch. I was pleased.

Mrs Ferguson's brother telephoned me daily for two weeks, barring weekends. He tried to persuade me that I would be a better person if I widened my sexual horizons and I loved him trying to persuade me. For two weeks I led him to believe that I might be persuaded because that is what I believed myself.

During those two weeks I was more affectionate than ever to George, who was very busy at work because there was a rush on and often home later than usual. I didn't compare him unfavourably with Mrs Ferguson's brother. I simply expected less of him. I was also extremely patient and sensitive to the needs of the children, who sometimes had to shout at me to get my attention but who were rewarded with kindness when they did. Having an admirer was good for me.

Two weeks after the retirement party he phoned and said he needed to talk to me desperately. 'As a friend,' I said.

'Sort of,' he replied.

We met in a park where he kissed me passionately, although I wanted to resist, and asked me not to torment him any longer. I told him I didn't want to torment him. He said I was. I said if that was the case I could never see him again. He said, 'Oh, well.' He didn't look too bothered for a man in torment. He said he was off to South America the next day. He would take his broken heart with him. I giggled all the way home, delighted with my success, over the moon that I had survived the encounter with a tiny amount of dignity and my virtue more or less intact. There's unfaithful in thought and word, I know. Jimmy Carter taught us that. But it's nothing like as serious as unfaithful in deed, and it feels fantastic.

George was late again that night. I began to wonder where he was. Mathesons weren't noted for their rushes.

'What are you rushing?' I asked the minute he walked through the door at half past seven.

'Some plans,' he said. 'The usual.'

I said nothing. I started listening. George, I decided was more talkative than usual and much of his conversation was peppered with news of a girl called Janey. Janey was the most intelligent girl in the office. She would go a long way. She had a terrible home life. Her father was violent. George felt sorry for her. My blood reacted to 'sorry'. I knew what 'sorry' meant.

'Which one is Janey?' I asked. 'What did she wear to the Ferguson's?'

'You wouldn't have noticed her,' he said. 'She's a plain little thing. Tiny and mousey.' But there had been no tiny, mousey girls at the Ferguson's. Only bosomy, blonde maneaters and me and Mrs Punnet.

Suspicion and jealousy are not easy to contain in the self-righteous breast. They give rise to anger and manslaughter. I was furious at George for waving the idiot Janey at me. I had given him no cause to be jealous. I had never once mentioned Mrs Ferguson's brother or sighed over his charms as George seemed to sigh over Janey's. I had never remarked on his golfing or his colouring or his home life. What had gone on between us had gone on in private. Out of deference to George and to protect our marriage I had put an end to the adoration before it amounted to anything. Why couldn't George do the same for me?

The delays at work continued. I was sure they were Janey. George was looking excessively well on his hard work. He walked with a spring in his step and apart from being an hour and a half late every night he was treating me with consideration I hadn't seen in years.

Guilt, I said to myself. The thought nibbled away at my trust and discretion and I knew it was only a matter of time before I would have to confront him with my belief in his infidelity. I began looking for evidence, smelling his shirts and rifling his pockets in search of tell-tale phone numbers and restaurant receipts. I found none.

I fired a warning shot. 'I remember Janey,' I said one day. 'Moustache Short, fat legs.'

Then help arrived from South America, a card in an envelope on which Mrs Ferguson's brother had written, 'If ever you change your mind, I will be waiting.'

'Who's that from?' George asked.

'Mrs Ferguson's brother,' I said.

'What's he want, writing to you?' There was surprise but no concern in his voice. It takes George a while to cotton-on.

'He says if I change my mind, he will be waiting.'

'About what?' he asked, putting down his spoonful of All-Bran. 'Change your mind about what?'

'Golf lessons,' I said. 'What do you think?' He sat at the table looking pained. He put out his hand for the card.

'What's been going on?' he said.

'Nothing,' I replied, giving it to him. 'As you can see. Nothing.' He read it and pushed away his cereal.

'I hope not,' he said. 'We have to trust each other, Tessa. You know that, don't you?' I said I did. I said I sometimes wondered if he did.

The rush stopped that very night, as did all mention of Janey. I don't know what was going on and I don't want to know but whatever it was, it was certainly a rush and I hope it was extremely uncomfortable.

I'm not sure what drove George to it. Not sex. It's never sex to begin with. Romance, I suppose. The same thing that tempted me. And vanity. I will always long for romance and a marriage like ours is probably the last place I'll find it. But I don't long for it as much as I value my marriage. And I don't suppose I ever will, not while Mrs Ferguson's brother stays in South America and hairy girls like Janey look to George for consolation.

CHAPTER FOURTEEN

Home of Horrors

George and I didn't hurry into home-ownership because he wanted to hurry into something modern and modest in a leafy suburb. I wanted to move into something run-down, round the corner, which we could restore lovingly and prudently to retain its charm, character and investment value. We waited for Christopher to try and throw himself out of our first floor flat through the sitting-room window before doing anything. He did this just before his fourth birthday. He was looking for someone to play with.

'He is trying to tell us something,' I said to George, who had caught him by the ankles.

'Why doesn't he just speak,' George replied. The shock had made him edgy. We began to discuss moving immediately but we couldn't get the discussion beyond the same old circle, which took us fifteen miles to the southwest.

George didn't just want a house. He wanted there to be nice neighbours, security, peace, friends for the children to grow up with and a garden. 'I don't want to live in a slum,' he said. 'I want a dining-room.' George took an O-level in dining-rooms. I told him. I said, 'Why are you so dumb and conventional?'

I said I couldn't bear to live in a rut and a rut was

what he had his eye on. He said it was all right for me.
I had grown up with open spaces around me. I said,
but I left them. He said, who was I thinking of myself
or the children and so on and so forth.

'Selfish?' I screamed at him one day as we sat on a
bench on the common watching the juggernauts belch-
ing pollution across the chic rows of terraces which
were beyond our means. 'Who's being selfish? I'm
settled here. I don't want to move out. I've got my job
and Floss and the nursery all within a mile of each
other. I like it here.'

'Keep your voice down,' he whispered. 'There are
other jobs, nurseries and child-minders.'

'And wives,' I said. 'You'd better start looking.'

'Tessa,' he said soothingly because he hates a public
spectacle, 'be reasonable. I'd never have expected you
to be so unadventurous.'

'Suffocation in the sticks is not my idea of a challenge,' I said sulkily. But I knew I had argued it
wrongly. I wouldn't have minded leaving the area one
bit if we had been moving further in. It wasn't leaving
the area that frightened me. It was the years I could see
stretching before me in a landscape which could easily
be mistaken for a still-life.

I began mooching around estate agent's windows,
staring at the local houses for sale which we couldn't
afford. George sneakily rang agents in suburbs he liked
and had them send their lists of houses, which we
often could afford and which didn't appear to be in
immediate danger of falling down. On the contrary,
many of them had lock-up garages. He said, wouldn't
I just go and look at them?

'Looking at them won't bring them any closer,' I
said.

Eventually I gathered enough courage to go into the
neighbourhood agents to tell them what I was looking
for. I tried to look respectable. I tried to look like a

property speculator though I felt Katy on my hip let me down. Especially the holes in her dungarees.

'I want something I can do up,' I explained. 'With a garden and not on a main road.' I told them how much I had to spend. They asked me if I had thought about moving out ten miles or so. I said they didn't have to be so snooty. I told them I used to work in an estate agents. They said they weren't being snooty. They were being realistic. I said it was people like them who had dragged the area down, arriving in droves to force the prices up.

Then I found a very old agency run by an ancient man called Bloom, who had worked there all his life and who seemed unaware of the inflation raging around him. He had the trust of families who hadn't moved in generations and though his houses weren't cheap either, he did have access to one or two bombsites he thought might interest me.

They were hideous. Dark, damp, cramped and rotten. I said that neither George nor I were insured against hypothermia and we had two small children. I asked George if we should think about emigrating. He said he didn't mind the idea of Australia with its space and sunshine. 'Not Australia,' I said. 'New York.' We were several thousand miles from a compromise.

I was wondering how we could best divide the children when Mr Bloom rang about the deceased estate. 'It's not very pretty,' he said. 'But it's in your price range and I don't suppose anyone else will want it.' Mr Bloom knew how to sell.

We met outside Mrs Sparrow's in a frantic storm, which showed it to its best advantage. I fell in love with it at once. It was in the middle of a terrace that several new owners had tried valiantly to restore and it stuck out like a thumb hanging by a thread. It looked like a house of horrors. Katy began to cry the minute we struggled in out of the rain.

Mr Bloom said, 'Can you blame her?' He was quick to point out all the obvious drawbacks: the holes in the roof, the derelict pointing, the disgraceful sanitation and the crumbling plaster.

'But it can all be fixed,' I said. 'Did Mrs Sparrow die of exposure?'

'No,' he said without flinching. 'She fell down the stairs and broke her neck.'

'It's the atmosphere that counts,' I said. 'And the potential.' Mrs Sparrow was so newly deceased that her atmosphere hung in the air where she had left it. Her linen was still in the cupboard and cutlery in the drawers, and in the wardrobe in her bedroom a row of grey and navy dresses fell empty from her coat-hangers.

'We'll buy it,' I said to Mr Bloom. 'It has a dining-room.'

'It has a dining-room,' I said to George, who stood outside it with tears in his eyes the following evening.

'No,' he moaned. 'No Tessa. It's out of the question.' It was a clear summer evening and the shadows fell flatteringly across the quaintly shaped rooms and the bijou portico. But he wasn't looking at the portico. He was glowering at the ugly grey building on the corner. 'What's that?' he barked.

'Squash courts,' I said. 'You won't even have to jog round the block for exercise.'

'Men my age have heart attacks playing squash,' he snarled. 'It looks bloody ugly.'

'Cosmopolitan is what it looks,' I said. But my stomach churned as George frowned at No 36 in a manner that I knew spelt trouble. He is an easy-going man until he turns his heart against something. As we surveyed the woodwork with its peeled paint, the bricks that had nothing between them to give you any confidence, the broken fence and the extraordinary angle of the front door, I could hear the ghastly grinding of his heart turning against the only house I had ever wanted in the whole world. All my life.

'Surely no one lives here,' he said.

'Not any more,' I said. 'But someone did until quite recently.'

'And where are they now?' he enquired. His voice squeaked with sarcasm.

'Dead.' I admitted. 'Which is just as well. You wouldn't want a sitting tenant. And if this wasn't a deceased estate it wouldn't be so cheap.' I hadn't told him about Mrs Sparrow because he is squeamish.

'If you are contemplating raising our children in this house you are even madder than you look,' he said.

I nagged and nagged all the way round the house, in and out of the sunlit-filled kitchen with its sweetly creaking floor, up the mahogany staircase which you could still see under layers of paint, in and out of the three bedrooms with their marvellously encrusted walls and back down to the two reception-rooms of cosy proportions and undeniably original ceilings. 'The dining-room,' I announced. 'Can't you see its potential?'

'I've seen enough,' he said. 'Let's go home.'

'The garden,' I cried. 'Not without seeing the garden. It has its own shed.'

'That is not a shed,' he snapped, wiping blood from the shin he had cracked on a raised flower bed. 'That is an outside lavatory.'

'It will convert,' I said. 'And you have to admit it's a pretty garden.' But he was admitting nothing.

A man from next door put his head over the wall. 'Shouldn't buy it if I were you,' he volunteered. 'Not with tragedy in it.'

'We won't be buying it,' George sniggered. 'What tragedy?'

'I don't know,' I said. 'We'll get the stairs seen to.'

I argued with George for two weeks and each day

142

called on Mr Bloom to make sure no one else was vying for it.

'Why would they?' he asked.

In the end I fell back on my old stand-bys: lies, deception and fraud, as well as George's frugal streak. First I had him admit that Mrs Sparrow's was cheaper than the crummiest villa he had been offered. Then I had him admit that his greatest fear was the expense involved in civilizing it and the time and the energy. Then I convinced him that I would take care of everything.

'Please, George, let me,' I begged. 'I've always wanted to. To prove myself. If I can organize the renovation of this house I will have proved myself.'

'Proved yourself what?' he asked with interest.

'Adequate,' I said. He shook his head. But I didn't give up. I assured him I would adhere to the strictest budget, find the best and cheapest workmen, learn about building and plumbing myself so I could oversee the work, and do the decorating myself.

'I know you think it's going to cost a fortune,' I said. 'But it won't. I'll make sure it doesn't. A lot of the work is just cosmetic.'

I don't know whether I convinced him or exhausted him but in the end he capitulated. 'All right, all right,' he cried at four one morning when I had woken him up to discuss commuting. 'Have your stinking house. Let me sleep.'

Mr Bloom was very helpful. He said we should get a surveyor's report because it was best to know the worst and he said he thought he might be able to arrange a mortgage. The surveyor's report was not helpful. It concluded with words to the effect that the house was a public menace, so I ignored it. I was able to ignore it because Mr Bloom's brother came up with the money.

You'd have thought our friends would have been

pleased. But they weren't. Mary Morley said, 'I wouldn't be you for anything,' and that she said outside.

Jennifer said, 'The children, Tessa. Think of the disease.'

My mother said, 'Oh, Tessa. Oh well.'

George's reservations, however, faded with time and the knowledge that he was on the brink of home-ownership and manhood. He even decided to show it to Hatty. I said I thought this could be a mistake but he wouldn't listen.

She made a funny noise as we pulled up outside and George told her this was it. I thought she was being sick but she was only saying 'urrrgh'.

'I know it's not much yet,' George apologized. 'But we have great plans for it.' I prayed she wouldn't ask what they were because I knew he didn't know.

'It's terrible,' she said. As we trooped through the kitchen to admire the garden George put his foot through the floor and sunk to his thigh. Hatty gave a small scream: 'Oh!' she screamed. 'Oh! The place is rotten.'

I laughed, musically. 'Only the floor,' I trilled. 'We knew about that. It's all in the surveyor's report.'

'I hope you know what you're doing, George, I really do,' his mother rasped.

'I know what I'm doing,' he whimpered. 'I'm trying to get out of this hole and no one will help me.'

There were other accidents which could best be described as unfortunate and which in no way alerted me to the enormity of my folly.

The man from the Public Health Department electro-cuted himself when he switched on the kitchen light. The ancient Ascot exploded when George tried to light it and the man next door, rushing into the street upon hearing the noise, said it was nothing short of a miracle that the whole row hadn't come down. When George's father, in a moment of quite uncalled for curiosity, pulled away a little of the paper in the hall to see what was underneath, a wall fell on top of him. But there were no fatalities and my faith in the house never wavered. If it wavered, I knew, everything would waver.

I pretended to myself that George's opposition had never been serious and that the limb I was out on wasn't riddled with dry-rot. I tried to ignore the question that echoed dangerously through the sleepless nights that suddenly beset me. It was the voice of Mrs Sparrow demanding an answer, 'Can a marriage support a crumbling house?' she wanted to know. 'Or a house a crumbling marriage?'

CHAPTER FIFTEEN

A Moving Experience

The removal men had the fridge stuck halfway down the stairs where they had already dropped a crate of fortified rabbits' livers when George asked for a divorce.

'I can't go on like this, Tessa,' he said. 'This isn't living.'

'It's moving,' I bawled. 'It's not my fault.'

'It's more than that,' he said. 'It's the way you go about things. I can't go on living with the way you go about things.'

'Keep packing,' I said.

I suppose it was Charlie and Ron, the removal men. And Herbie the builder and Mick the electrician and the living-room wall that had disintegrated along with all hope of a dining-room. In showing George what I could do with Mrs Sparrow's house I had revealed to him my true nature and he found it shocking. My true nature turned out to be very, very unlucky. George did not think this attractive.

A marriage has to be structurally sound to withstand the tension of house renovation. Ours had begun with shaky foundations and as soon as we completed the transaction on the deceased estate, subsidence set in. The solid walls we had spent so many years building started to shift and slide dangerously. On moving day it looked like collapsing altogether.

Charlie and Ron found the movement absorbing. They would stop and listen in between trips up and down the stairs with the contents of our flat. 'Why blame me?' I shouted. 'You were there. Can't you speak?'

'What good would that have done?' George replied. 'When has speaking ever had any effect on you?'

'The trouble isn't me or the house,' I cried. 'It's you. You can't stand the change. That's what it is.'

'Maybe. Maybe. But I can't take any more. I'll get you into the house and then I'll leave.'

'Er, Tessa,' said Charlie. 'I don't want to butt in. But the bed's bust. Will we move it or leave it where it is to save space on the truck?'

George said, 'Oh, my God. This is the worst day of my life.'

'Load it, Charlie,' I said wearily. 'We'll deal with it later.'

I thought I sounded a bit like Miss Ellie, bravely and calmly dealing with disasters while running the estate and planning breakfast. It was a role I had come to relish in a few longish months. Although I had had to confront catastrophe after catastrophe making our home habitable, I loved being in charge. George, however, had become a bitter man, bitter and withdrawn.

'OK,' I told him one evening. 'You take over. You do better.' But he refused. He said, how could he? Where would he find the time?

'You got us into this mess,' he whined. 'How can I stop you making it messier?' He said this the night I told him Herbie had knocked down the living-room wall, although no one had asked him to. He had

149

totally lost confidence in me. My own confidence in me wasn't all that secure any more either.

'It was a weak wall,' I tried to explain. 'It just fell down the minute they leant on it.' Part of my function, as I saw it, was to defend the workers I employed no matter how enormous their blunders. I had to defend them because I was responsible for them. I tried to understand them. That's how innocent I was.

'What did you knock the wall down for, Herbie?' I asked.

'You wanted it down, didn't you?' he replied. 'Everyone gets rid of that wall.'

'No,' I said. 'We wanted to keep that wall.'

'But that's silly,' he protested. 'Look at the size of the rooms. I mean, people have cupboards this size. Last week I built cupboards this size for a woman up in Stockwell.'

I said to George, 'It would have been a very small dining-room. What we will now have is an enormous living-room. Be grateful for an enormous living-room.'

'You'll have to make them rebuild it in their own time,' George said.

'You tell them that,' I said.

'No, this is your house, Tessa,' he brayed. 'You fix it.' But I didn't fix it because I knew Herbie would walk off the job the minute I told him to put the wall back and then I would have to pay someone else to rebuild it and that would cost money I didn't have.

I don't know why I remained loyal to Herbie for as long as I did. He had come from a leaflet shoved through the door and he told me he had the best men working for him in the whole of South London. 'I mean that, Tessa,' he'd said, casting his crooked eye over Mrs Sparrow's house. 'A better lot of lads you'll never find.' And I'd believed him. I couldn't think of any reason not to. Normal people don't lie.

150

With hindsight, I can see that Herbie wasn't normal. It wasn't just his perfectly square head, it was his criminal tendencies. The way he came by the scaffolding, for one thing, didn't seem entirely honest and what he charged me for the roof certainly wasn't.

'I don't think I want to hear this,' I said of the scaffolding.

'Quite right, Tessa, quite right,' he chortled. 'But these are the risks I'm prepared to take for you. I know money doesn't grow on trees.'

George, who was more experienced than me in workmen on account of the car, might have suspected Herbie before I did. But he didn't have much to do with him because he came to the house as little as possible. I gave him progress reports: 'Herbie says he's never seen anything like the floor joists.' But these just made him tremble. The only things that really concerned him were the bank stubs and for these he blamed me, not Herbie.

I don't think Herbie minded not seeing George. He liked dealing with a woman struggling to make her first house safe and warm for her family. He was supposed to replace the roof, the kitchen floor, the wiring and to install central heating. Herbie saw me coming.

He took a month over the roof, although the weather was clear and the roof small. He suggested I pay him weekly, which he said was better in the long run and he made it the longest-running roof repair in the history of slates.

His plumber had a lot of trouble with the central heating pipes because of the floor. That's what he told me. 'The floor,' I said to George, who put his head in his hands. Herbie had me over the usual barrel of ignorance and the only defence I had was suspicion.

I was at the house when he brought in his electrician. 'This is Mick,' he said. 'I'm just taking him over the place.' Herbie took the lead, followed by Mick and I brought up Mick's rear, which I could see plainly through his ripped overalls. It was very white. I stared at it in fascination and thought, 'This is what it is like in a man's world.'

Herbie told Mick he would laugh his head off when he saw what had to be done. Mick looked at the prehistoric plugs and the semi-modernized sockets and the congested fuse box and he did, he laughed his head off.

'We'll have to have the lot out,' he said. 'It's going to cost you a packet.'

Herbie sighed in sympathy. 'It's your money or your life though, isn't it? That's what I always say.' When Mick had gone I told Herbie I wanted a second opinion. I said the surveyor's report hadn't said complete rewiring. It had said partial rewiring.

Herbie remarked that surveyors were a lying lot who didn't know a wire from a dog's hair and that in his opinion Mick was the best there was, but because another man was what I wanted, and it was his job to please the customer, another man was what I would have. I waited for him for two weeks and then complained. Herbie said, 'Look, love. I'm losing money on this job as it is. If you want another bleeding electrician, you get one.' I sensed he was losing interest.

A week before we were due to move in, he took off, having finished the roof and the plumbing but leaving floorboards stacked against the walls and more holes than floor to walk on. The living-room was piled high with rubble. We had to hire a skip to clear it out ourselves. I suppose he had deduced after years of practice and from watching my face grow more and more haggard with every passing trip to the bank that we had run out of money.

The Richardsons, who lived four doors along, suggested the electrician and the carpenter who finally made our house safe. They had been watching the growing chaos with interest and relief that it wasn't theirs. 'It's awful, isn't it?' Pam said over the gate. 'But it will probably be worth it.'

George didn't care about what the Richardsons thought. He had come to believe that anyone who lived in the street was insane. He wasn't impressed when I told him Pam was a caterer and had a big dining-room. I didn't mention the grant for the roof she told me we were entitled to because it was too late to claim it and his heart might have stopped irreparably.

By the time we came to move in, the house looked very little different from when we had first seen it. There was a new roof, which you had to cross the road to see, safe wires and plugs, which did nothing to improve the walls, a solid kitchen floor already covered in grime, and heating, but it was summer.

My enthusiasm for it had tarnished and the trust George had placed in me to hand out limited funds wisely had disintegrated. The night before the move we sat among the debris of our flat, which no longer looked like home, and we stared at each other in dismay. I hadn't seen George look so miserable since our wedding night.

'This is the stupidest thing I have ever done,' he moaned.

'Stop moaning,' I snapped. 'It's done now. Just put up with it for a bit and you'll get to love it. Think of the garden.'

Thinking of the garden gave him insomnia. At two o'clock in the morning he said suddenly, 'They are proper removalists aren't they, Tessa? They won't break anything, will they?'

'They're insured,' was all I was prepared to say.

Charlie and Ron didn't come personally recommended either. Personally recommended movers were several hundred pounds more expensive. They advertised in the local paper: 'Speedy removals! Cheap rates!' What more could you want? I suppose a proper removal van would have been a bonus. Charlie and Ron had a kind of pickup truck which they said made loading and unloading easier. I said, 'What happens if it rains?'

'We drive faster,' Charlie laughed. I thought he was joking.

George clutched his chest when he saw the truck. 'Are you crazy?' he hissed at me in the bathroom, where he had dragged me for privacy. 'You don't move house in an open truck.'

'Don't panic,' I urged. 'It's too late to get anything else now, anyway.'

There was no chance of a postponement because our landlord had arranged for his new tenants to move in that afternoon and I'd assured him that we would be out by lunchtime. Charlie had assured me this was no problem. 'There's nothing here to give us any bother,' he said on arrival.

'Only my husband,' I laughed.

'Yeah?' he said blankly. Charlie and I didn't understand each other's jokes, I thought at the time. Later I realized no one had made any jokes.

By two o'clock George was demanding a divorce and the new people had started to move in. As we passed each other on the stairs I heard George mutter, 'Ghouls.' The woman who was the new tenant looked at him in astonishment. She was carrying only her handbag and leading a long line of neatly uniformed men who were moving her pristine furniture in an orderly manner. She stopped and said in a voice which carried to the fifth floor, 'You have left the place like a pig-sty.'

I rushed down the stairs disguised as a duvet to cover my embarrassment. I hadn't had time to clear seven years of filth from places that had been covered by fixed objects like the watering-can and the tennis racquets.

We finally locked ourselves into Mrs Sparrow's at 6 p.m., looking like refugees from a fire in a tip. I remembered too late that I had left our spade and some nails and some broken china George's mother had given us in a cupboard in the lobby. George said he couldn't care less. He collapsed in despair on our sofa, which had been torn in transit. I knew that the time had come to try to restore our foundations.

'If I go back and get the spade and nails we could do some underpinning,' I said to George.

He said, 'What's that?'

'I don't know,' I confessed. 'But it sounds friendly.' He managed a sickly grin. We left the children where they were for the night, which was with Hatty, who was seriously considering having them made wards of the court until we moved again. I made a cup of tea in our new home with its safe wiring, new floor and sturdy roof and I said to George, 'We had better put it back on the market if you want a divorce.'

He spat his tea out because the cup was filled with wood shavings and said, 'No one would buy it. We were fools.' We looked out on to the garden where the sun shone on the broken paving and the roses bloomed regardless. Then we wandered around the house together and I said, 'At least it's ours.'

'Oh, God,' he groaned. 'That's what I can't stand.'

But he came to stand it and now that we have had several hundred other workmen in to do what they can with the place he has come to love it, not because it is so vastly improved but because of the time it has taken. All he ever needed was time.

He loves the garden. It's small enough for him to

weed and large enough for him to mow and on a windy day when the trees opposite are in full flight it's even leafy. As for me, I love being in the thick of things, even though the only truly thick thing round here is the pollution. We both complain from time to time but it's been a fairly happy compromise and the house, like the marriage, has yet to come tumbling down.

CHAPTER SIXTEEN

Snappy Shots

The charm of family holidays is remembering them. You have them to remember as the years go by and to sigh over because they are the good times. They are also refresher courses for fathers who kid themselves that they are family men for fifty weeks of the year. This is why they are always hell to begin with.

The very first holiday we ever took as a family began with an emergency stop on the M5 and Christopher screaming blue murder because Katy had been sick on him. Katy is not a good traveller. She gets this from George's side of the family. George likes to pretend she is a good traveller. He says, 'Stop fussing. She's only sick because you put it into her head.' He says this because he knows she gets it from him and he imagines that if she isn't sick he won't be either. But he was once sick on a becalmed pedalo and Katy hadn't even been born.

Christopher screamed, 'I stink. Get it off. Look at my feet.' He can always be counted on to draw attention to himself in a crisis. George says this is from my side.

We were on our way to a seaside bungalow in Devon owned by a friend of my brother Nick. I don't know why we expected to enjoy ourselves. It wasn't a high point in our marriage. George was under a great deal of strain

158

because of the house and I was under the strain of George's strain and also the strain of the house.

We were being held together by a workable routine which the holiday simply broke and we were in no mood for full-time exposure to each other's shortcomings, let alone the shortcomings of the unfamiliar territory we were supposed to unwind in. Katy probably threw up because of the tension.

Nick had said we would be mad if we didn't go. 'You sound as if you're a hundred,' he said. The friend was called Trojan and the bungalow was going cheap.

'No one is called Trojan,' I said.

'His real name is Don,' Nick agreed.

'And bungalows by the sea don't go cheap in July.'

'Cheap for friends,' he explained.

So we took it. I talked to Trojan, who seemed more or less normal on the phone and who told me he was managing the bungalow for his parents who were abroad. They wanted it occupied but he couldn't be relied on to be there all the time, he said. He didn't want to charge extortionate rents, he just wanted it occupied. That was why it was cheap.

'He is a very nice, honest man,' I said to George, and he took my word for it. Trojan turned out to be as honest as Herbie and as nice as a cold-sore. He was there to greet us when we arrived and he looked more or less normal for a man who had changed his name from Don. Appearances are only there to deceive us.

'Hi,' he called as he crossed the neat lawn to the carport. 'I thought I'd drop by with some supplies.'

'I hope he's not going to hang around,' George muttered.

'Why should he?' I muttered back.

'It's just a few groceries and vegetables and things,' Trojan said easily, ruffling Christopher's hair and admiring Katy's bucket. His smile wasn't the smile of a cheat or a freeloader. He gave George a bill for £30 for the provisions, which George paid immediately. They turned out to be mainly bottles of Hoi-Sin sauce and Chinese mushrooms.

'What did you pay him for?' I shouted at George.

'To get rid of him,' he snapped. But it took more than £30 to get rid of Trojan. He was back a few hours later to see if we were all right and to join us for supper, borrow the shower and spend the night on the sofa, provided we didn't mind. We were in no position to mind. The rent was low and we were there as friends.

'You'll have to tell him to go,' I hissed at George when we were in bed, rigid with anger and exhaustion at one in the morning.

'He's your brother's friend,' he replied. He said he wanted to go home. I said we all wanted to go home but we had to be grown up about it. The holiday was for the children. He slammed his foot against the end of the bed. 'Them!' he cried.

Trojan wasn't there for breakfast. 'We misjudged him,' I said with relief.

'We didn't,' George said. His instinct for man's baseness had been finely honed by the builders. He reappeared at lunch just as George was taking his food to the far end of the garden because he said he couldn't stand the children's table manners.

'They are the same table manners they have in London,' I called after him. 'Oh. Hullo, Trojan.' He was still there when we came back from the beach at tea.

'Tell him to leave,' I said to George again.

'How can I,' he replied, 'when you have asked him to stay for supper?'

'Just say we want to be alone.'

'But you've already asked him to stay.'

'Pretend you don't know. Pretend I haven't told you. Tell him I've got a disease.'

'Tessa,' George said. 'Drop dead.'

I can really only describe the temper he was in as

foul. He looked with amazement on the children and expressed disbelief at the irritating habits they had, like breathing and being there. It wasn't just Trojan. He simply wasn't used to day-long fatherhood. He was used to them being there for two pleasant hours at a time, bathed, fed and ready for bed. He decided it was Christopher's fault that Trojan wouldn't go away.

'He's like you,' he said. 'He latches on to people.'

'I don't latch on to people,' I said. 'I just get on with them. Christopher wouldn't get on so well with Trojan if you played with him more. Trojan's probably lonely.'

'Lonely, my foot,' George said. 'He's using us.'

'Christopher's using him,' I said. 'In the absence of any other obvious father.'

George said, 'This is my holiday. I want to relax.'

I said, 'And it's my holiday.' But he pretended he didn't hear and I didn't repeat it because it was starting to sound as if neither of us wanted the children, who hadn't asked to come in the first place, or even be born.

I know better now, after several more family holidays. I know now that it's a simple matter of adjustment. But I didn't then. Then, I began to wonder how I could organize a drowning.

The minute we hit the beach George threw himself on to his back and went to sleep, even though he had just finished sleeping for ten hours in bed. I built the sandcastles, threw the ball, jumped the waves and queued for the donkey until I could stand it no longer. This took three whole days. Then I screeched the full length of the sandy, white beach, 'It's your turn now. Get up and be a father or I will go and get Trojan.'

He slept on, feigning death on account of his embarrassment. 'Daddy, Mummy's talking to you,' Christopher screamed. Katy jumped on to his stomach. He sat up and laughed agreeably for the spectators but I knew there would be trouble. He ground my sunglasses into the sand as he scrambled to his feet. He ignored me as

I slumped to my bit of the towel and, tucking a child under either arm, he rushed to the water with them laughing and squealing and carrying on as if he was their favourite parent.

He didn't come back to the umbrella. He took them for a long walk, gathering shells and looking at seaweed and girl's backs and fronts. When Katy grew tired he put her on his shoulders like a model father. He was gone so long that I had every chance to hear the life story of the single mother next bucket along.

I didn't latch on to her. I simply smiled at her baby. Who wouldn't, in the absence of her own? She said it wasn't too bad being a single mother, just lonely and exhausting. I said I knew. She said, how could I when I had a husband as handsome and helpful as George. I said, George who? She said her baby was hyperactive, though she didn't look too hyperactive to me. She was sitting peacefully on a towel eating sand. 'Drugged,' the mother laughed. I laughed too, though I wasn't sure why.

All the time she was talking I kept my eyes on my family, who were rollicking along the beach in a manner so carefree that I wondered if they could truly be mine. 'I envy you,' the single mother said. 'I mean, we're not exactly a family.' I was aware of a small sensation in the corners of my mouth that felt like smiling. I was smiling gratefully. I asked the single mother to supper. I told her to bring her hyperactive child. By the time George returned with his eyes devoid of any recognition of the moments of passion and love we had once shared, it was too late to uninvite her.

I tried to sound as if we were fond of each other and deserving of her envy. 'Darling,' I gushed. 'This is Judith. I've asked her to supper tonight. She doesn't know anyone and I thought it would be fun.'

George didn't look at Judith. He looked at me and said

in a voice which he squeezed from its horrible little box, 'But surely we've got Trojan coming already.'

'So we have,' I giggled. 'Isn't that lucky?'

We left the beach shortly afterwards, having given Judith simple directions to our bungalow and suggesting she arrive at seven. George and I strode home in silence, pausing only to check the garden for signs of Trojan before locking ourselves in to do battle.

'Why are you doing this to me, Tessa? Is it punishment?' he asked.

'Punishment for what?' I said, throwing wet and sandy clothes into the sink.

'For being mean about the children. I admit I was mean about the children.'

'Thank you,' I said. 'I'm not punishing you.'

'Then why have you asked this woman to supper when there's already Trojan? You know how I hate strange people.'

'She isn't strange,' I said. 'She is a single mother. And you weren't just mean about the children. You were disgusting to me.'

'If it comes to that, Tessa,' he began. But it didn't come to that because Katy waddled in carrying a box of matches and Christopher called from the garden, 'Come and see what I've done.' He had set fire to the carport. I screamed and ran to save him. George rushed for the garden hose and doused the flames before they reduced the structure to a charred mess. Trojan bowled up as we stood surveying the damage. He looked at the carport and looked at the children. 'I lit the carport,' Christopher told him. 'You should've seen it.'

Trojan was persuaded to stay for supper and took George out to the back to talk about compensation. Judith arrived with her child, who was yelling her head off just as I heard George say, 'I could build three new ones for that, and a house.'

The baby continued to yell all night even though I

walked it round and round the garden and showed it the burnt remains over and over again because Judith was too preoccupied with Trojan to pacify it. When I thought I was about to drop from fatigue George came out to find me. 'They don't look like going home,' he said. 'Go and tell them to go home.'

'You,' I said. 'I'm out here holding the baby.' He must have, because within a very minutes Trojan was escorting Judith to the gate and assuring us that he would see her home safely.

'What about the baby?' I said.

'Sorry,' said Judith. 'I almost forgot her.'

While we were washing up I said to George, 'You can't take your eyes off Christopher for a minute.'

'Or Katy,' he agreed. And we didn't for the rest of our holiday. George continued to go to sleep the minute he fell on to the sand but he faithfully took them for a walk each afternoon after lunch while I read. 'Don't talk to anyone,' he said every day.

We watched with fascination as Christopher made friend after friend with no trouble at all because that is how he is, and as Katy allowed a dozen or so other hefty toddlers to run off with her ball and made no attempt to reclaim it because that is how she is. 'They are wonderful,' George said.

We didn't see any more of Judith or Trojan until the day we left and he came to settle up. 'The deposit will cover the carport,' he said generously.

'Three times over,' George laughed. This is how relaxed he had become. He was now a man who could relax over money down the drain. There are photos in our album of the holiday and on it we are all looking happy. They were taken in the second week when we were used to each other and the shortcomings were few and far between.

CHAPTER SEVENTEEN

No One's Perfect

Acceptance is the first rule of survival in marriage. Some people call it resignation. It means putting up with faults that on a bad day have you reaching for your passport or the axe. How quickly you reach this benumbed state depends pretty well on how bad the faults are and how wise and perceptive you are and desperate not to be thrown out on to the street.

George has never come to terms with my 'lying', as he calls it. He has never grasped the fact that it has absolutely nothing to do with malicious deception. And I will never understand his irrational passion for objects. It seems ridiculous to me that an easy-going man can rise like a mighty, outraged beast from the depths of his sloth over things as cold-blooded as a camera or a car. But he does. These are not the least of our faults but they are among the most troublesome.

They were the root cause of a screaming match that briefly severed all links with George's mother and for one heady minute looked like severing the marital knot altogether, although it had been growing tighter for eight years or more. The straws that do most damage to the standard marriage's back are always insignificant, except in the cases of adultery, fraud and grievous bodily harm, which weren't issues at the time I am recalling.

I'm talking about the days immediately before Christopher's fifth birthday, which were untroubled days, carefree days, days for looking hopefully ahead – which I failed to do for one split second and a driver with a pinhead pulled up short on his way into a roundabout causing my car – George's car – to run into his. I saw straight away he wasn't a man who might put in a good word for me and save me from my husband's wrath.

He climbed out on to the roundabout, to the consternation of the seven million people behind us trying to get home for supper before midnight, and screeched into my window, 'A bloody woman. I might have known it. They never watch where they're going.' He seemed to be addressing God, whom he undoubtedly thought was on his side.

'Sorry,' I said. This was a reflex action.

'Sorry!' he shouted, delighted to have found someone so feeble to jump up and down on. 'I should think you're sorry. Look at the state of your car.' I staggered out and looked. The front was completely stoved in. I looked for signs of injury to his. There were none. The queue behind us began to remonstrate noisily, 'Pull over to the side,' he ordered. 'Come on. Hurry up.'

We exchanged names and addresses and licence numbers and insurance details. 'I don't know why you need to know my insurers,' I said weakly. 'There's not a mark on your car.'

'Not that we can see in this light,' he agreed. 'But I'm not taking any chances.' He drove off, pleased with himself and I returned to console my two dazed children. We struggled home with bits of metal dropping off all the way.

'Never mind,' I kept saying. 'It's going to be all right.' But I knew there was no easy way to break news of a tragedy to the next of kin, especially when the next of kin prides himself on never having had an accident in his life and wields his chamois leather with love and pride

167

on Sundays. I rehearsed phrases like, 'He was enormous' and, 'I think I blacked out,' but they weren't required.

A hideous silence led George into the house. 'What's happened to the car?' he shouted as soon as he clapped eyes on me hiding in the oven. 'What have you done to it?'

'I haven't done anything to it,' I said as fiercely as I could manage. 'A man stopped in front of me on a roundabout.'

'And you ran into him,' George shrieked. George becomes soprano when he is angry. The higher his pitch the more dangerous he is. I picked up Katy to protect myself. He wouldn't hit a mother with a baby, I thought. 'Were the children in the car?' he squealed.

'They don't normally run behind,' I said.

'Don't try and be funny, Tessa,' he squeaked. 'You have not only written off our car when we have no money at all, you have very nearly written off the children.' I knew he didn't care about the children but they lent weight to his hysteria.

'Oh, shut up,' I said and burst into tears. 'It wasn't my fault.'

'It's never your fault,' he said, unmoved. 'Whenever you do something really stupid, it is never your fault. What are we going to do for a car now? Tell me that! Where will we get the money to repair it?'

'Insurance,' I said. 'That's what insurance is for.'

'And lose my no-claims bonus?' His voice was so high now only dogs could hear it. I waited for a horde to stampede over the garden fence. 'Have you any idea how much my no-claims bonus is worth?' He stood in silence, waiting for me to guess, and while he was waiting he was struck by a realization so horrible he could hardly bring himself to utter it. 'What about the other driver?' he gasped. 'What about him?'

'A write-off,' I blubbed. 'Squashed to pieces.'

'Oh, no,' he said. 'Not dead.'

'Just the car,' I said. He collapsed on to the table, a wreck of a man. He didn't move. He appeared to be paralysed. 'Are you paralysed?' I enquired.

'I don't think you appreciate what you have done,' he said, slowly hauling himself to his feet so he could drag himself up to the bedroom and die in agony of an idiot wife. 'You simply have no idea.'

'Of course I have some idea,' I called after him, no longer tearful. I was suddenly fed up, which I always become when his concern for the inanimate gets to this stage. 'I was there. There wasn't a mark on the other car. I was only joking.'

'Joking,' he repeated. 'Joking.' I ran past him to avoid his coronary eyes and submerged myself in the children, where I stayed for several days because they saw nothing to forgive. He didn't lose all his no-claims bonus and the car was only off the road for a week but he was badly shaken by the incident. It was as if part of him had died. His front bumper. Time, I told myself, is a great healer. He will forget in time. But Time didn't get much of a chance.

Two weeks after the car was returned to us good as new – as new as a second-hand Ford Escort can ever be – I was driving down a very narrow lane behind the post office when a post office van approached me and stopped. The driver waved me forward, implying with all sorts of gestures and grimaces that if I couldn't get through the space he was allowing I didn't deserve to be behind the wheel of a car.

So I drove forward and within a very few life-recalling seconds I was wedged firmly against a skip. 'Heaven's a bleedin' bove,' called the van driver. 'What have you done?' His face was directly above mine, peering down from his window.

'What have *you* done?' I yelled at him. '*You* were the one who waved me forward.'

'But I cannot steer for you, madam,' he said. I put my foot on the accelerator, wishing only to leave the scene as quickly as possible. There was a fearful grinding of skip against Ford Escort – George's Ford Escort – and I was free. I didn't stop to consult further with the van driver who, like the pinhead, was untouched. I just headed home, deciding on the way that I would pretend it hadn't happened. I wouldn't tell George and I wouldn't even think about it. It was just possible it had never happened. I didn't even look for the damage when I parked the car. What I didn't know about, I told myself, I couldn't admit to.

George didn't stop to kiss the car that night on his way in so he didn't notice the large gash along the side until the following morning when he walked past it on the way to the bus stop. I heard his feet running back up the path and his fist go into spasm as it hammered on the door. I wondered if I could make a quick escape through the kitchen window. 'What's up?' I said. 'Are you sick?'

'Sick,' he moaned. 'I'm more than sick. Have you seen the car? What have you done to the car?'

'What do you mean, what have I done to the car? I've done nothing to the car. I'm not even dressed.'

'There is a dent in it. A great big dent in it, all along the passenger door. You must have done it.'

'I didn't do it,' I said. 'Someone has done it while it was parked.'

'The passenger door is to the kerb,' he yelped.

'Well it wasn't yesterday when I went to Safeway,' I said.

He came in and sat down, then he leapt up again and went to work saying, 'I think you should seriously consider never driving again.' I swallowed the insult thinking if that was the worst thing he was going to say I could handle it. But it wasn't. I'd been seen.

Tom Richardson from four doors along saw it all and meeting George on the bus that morning, reported the lot. 'Saw your wife having a run in with a skip by the post office,' he reported. You can't rely on anyone to keep their eyes closed.

George didn't come back to assault me or even phone to threaten me so I went through the day in carefree ignorance, bouncing happily about the health centre with a conscience as light as air. I was pleased I hadn't told him about the skip. It was bad enough having him suffer over the dent without me having to suffer as well. Him knowing I had done it would have made no difference to the dent or to the skip but it would make a large difference to peace in our time.

I even called in on Hatty at her dress shop to collect the family heirloom she wanted Christopher to have for his birthday next day. It was a cup George had drunk from as a boy with a dog on it. 'As we're not invited on the day itself,' she said, 'I'd like you to give it to him for us.'

George stormed in to confront me with my lie and my very limited future as a wife. 'Why did you lie?' he demanded. 'What sort of woman are you?' I told him it did him no good knowing and that I had been trying to avoid the scene we were now having.

'The scene we are now having is over your lying,' he yelled.

'Well the other scene then,' I said. 'Scene Two. Why I should be banned from driving.'

'And you should be,' he said. 'But the lies! The lying is unforgivable. You need to see a psychiatrist.'

'Leave me alone,' I screamed at him. 'You pious little twerp. I don't care about your car. I never want to drive your car again. I didn't crash it deliberately. The reason I have had two very small accidents in the last month is because I have so much on my mind. You try driving about with as much on my mind as I've got.'

'You are mad,' he said.

'*You* are mad,' I cried. 'With your insane obsession for things. I don't give a fig for things. And I don't want our

171

children to give a fig for things either.' So saying, I threw the wrapped cup with the dog on it at the sitting-room wall and killed it.

Because it was his son's birthday next day, George didn't leave home in anger. He stayed in bitter silence. I didn't tell Christopher about the cup immediately because I hadn't decided how to. It's all very well to admit a huge fault but how can you without it becoming a very bad example? Hatty rang before I'd worked it out. She rang to be thanked.

'Do you like the cup?' she asked Christopher.

'What cup?' he said. 'Mum, Granma said to give me the cup.'

'Oh, God,' I said.

George went to the phone like a condemned man. 'We couldn't give Christopher the cup, Mum,' he said. I held my breath, waiting for the full fury of the Wood family to descend upon me and devour me. 'There was a bit of an accident. I dropped it. Of course it broke,' he said. Then, 'Well it was my cup . . . Look Mum, it doesn't matter. It was my cup. I broke it. Now it's no one's cup . . . I don't think a twenty-five-year-old cup is all that important to a five-year-old boy . . . I'm sorry you feel like that . . . No . . . Right, then . . . Goodbye.'

I kissed George and said to Christopher, 'Sorry about the cup. We'll buy you another one.'

'I'd rather have the money,' he said. George rolled his eyes.

We never discussed the lie to his mother and we scarcely mentioned the car. We just picked up where we left off, trying to accept each other and resign ourselves to the faults that will never go away, no matter how long we are married.

CHAPTER EIGHTEEN

Marital Tumour

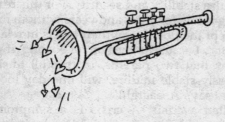

Children require stability and security. For this reason raising them goes on for years and years without much changing except the position of their heads in relation to their parents'. Because it goes on for so long, it very often happens that two parents, in the full flush of their relentlessly stable midlife, will one day look at each other and say, 'Aaaaargh!'

This is called a crisis. A crisis is a symptom of personal growth, the common or garden marital tumour that can be benign or malignant depending on the conditions. George and I had one last summer.

It didn't happen overnight. George started it two years ago when he suddenly glimpsed life beyond the telly. He had been a happy man, a contented man, a man prepared to wait for death rooted to the spot, but he looked out the window and cried, 'This can't go on. There must be more.' And he went out and bought a trumpet. I added to it by taking an O-level in maths, which went straight to my ambition. What brought it to its head was the inevitable conflict of interests. At the bottom of it, however, was the disappearance of our youth and the distant sighting of lost opportunities.

I greeted the trumpet with all the warmth of a bag of

party ice. 'Thirty-five pounds?' I yelled at him. 'You spent thirty-five pounds on a trumpet. You're not even musical. The down-pipe carries a tune better.'

This didn't touch him. 'We don't have thirty-five pounds to spend on personal luxuries,' I insisted. 'The children will have to go naked.'

'I have always wanted a trumpet,' he said. 'There is more to life than working, eating and sleeping. Time is slipping by.' He had seized the moment, he said, when he was offered the trumpet by a fellow at work and a book on how to play it. 'I'm thirty, Tessa.'

'Great,' I snapped. 'Provided you are happy. That is important. You are thirty and your life is slipping by. But just for the record, there is more to my life than working, sleeping and eating. There is cooking, washing, shopping, ironing, bathing the children, taking the children to and from school and listening to your boring moaning. I would love to have time to learn the trumpet. You don't know how lucky you are to have the time, not to mention the thirty-five quid.'

'Oh, God, the martyr's litany,' he groaned. 'I can't stand it.' It is one of the festering pustules of our marriage that George thinks my recitation of The Things I Do is a cheap trick, never to be taken seriously. But sometimes I can't help falling back on it, and I panicked at the sight of the trumpet.

I knew what it meant. Going through a marriage hand-in-hand is all very well to a point but when the point is reached, someone breaks into a run. I could see George running, with his trumpet, and I was terrified of being left behind, even though George is not a running man.

He had warned me, I realized. He had said only weeks before that he felt his life lacked something and I'd said did he mean a video. He'd said, 'Seriously, Tessa' before nodding off and I'd fantasized briefly about a life spinning on a houseboat in a mountain stream before turning off the television and forgetting about it.

When I recovered from the shock of the purchase I decided a trumpet was a lucky escape. He might have wanted to bicycle to New Guinea or take us all caving. I incorporated his trumpet playing into my image of him. He became George, my husband, the lovable automaton with a taste for jazz, even though it took him several months to master 'The Bluebells of Scotland'. If I moaned about him disappearing every Friday night for his lesson and leaving me with the washing-up, I was still relieved. If I thought, underneath it all, that there was something disgustingly self-indulgent about the way he cleaned the stupid thing, I only ever told Jennifer, Meg and Mary Morley. I never resented it, but he liked to think I did.

Several times a week he withdrew to the bathroom where he would practise. 'Shut up,' I would yell. 'Katy has just gone to sleep.' Mostly he would pretend he hadn't heard me but if his lip wasn't in he would appear at the top of the stairs.

'You give me no encouragement at all,' he would shout down in an effort to stir the sleeping child and teach me a lesson. 'You resent my trumpet.'

'I don't resent your trumpet,' I would squawk in a whisper. 'I resent the noise it makes at this time of night.'

He never talked about personally growing but it was clear that he liked the progress he was making and the confirmation that life wasn't hopeless, even at his age. He never said what caused him to notice time slipping by but I have tried to put myself in his place. I think he looked at me and Christopher and Katy and was overpowered by the sensation of being trapped by a nagging wife and two snotty children who were sucking him dry of his life's blood. I asked him once.

'Did you buy the trumpet because you have a

nagging wife and two snotty children draining you of your life force?' I enquired.

'No,' he said.

It took a year for me to decide to strike out on my own behalf and I can say, hand on heart, that embarking on my maths O-level wasn't an act of revenge. It was George who suggested it. He said he was sick of being married to a non-achiever. This was his idea of a joke. I said, 'I knew your education would get the better of you and you would come to despise me.'

He said, 'I don't despise you. I just want you to leave me alone.' He said this because I had taken to solving problems that didn't exist, like Christopher's loneliness, Katy's deafness and George's sleeping sickness. I was upsetting the family with my ruthless analysis of what had to be done for everyone to be perfect and everyone hated my idea of perfection. I was also bitterly resentful of the women I met who were making a success of their lives with careers and hobbies as well as children. George finally said, 'For God's sake! Take an O-level or something.'

I don't think he knew what he was saying. Certainly he had no idea of the consequences. Nor did I. To begin with I had to be dragged kicking and screaming to the classes because I was terrified of failure and other people's judgment. It took a full term for me to realize I was enjoying myself and that I actually liked going out on Monday nights to do the work I'd found so loathsome at school.

Sitting the exam was the most traumatic event of my intellectual life. It was the first event of my intellectual life. And there was nothing to compare with the misery of waiting for my result except for the extreme joy of learning I had passed with a flying colour. George said, 'A "B"? I only got a "C".' The information puzzled him. I was exhilarated by it. There is nothing quite so fine as knowing you aren't stupid on paper.

Jennifer, who had gone back to being a management consultant, although it has been her ruin, looked at me as a better-than-hopeless case. 'Get a few more O's and a couple of A's,' she advised, 'and I'll find a career for you.' Knowing Jennifer's taste it will probably be something in purple vinyl but I was pleased she suggested it.

I passed the plan on to George, who was less than enthusiastic. 'What's wrong with where you are?' he asked, referring to the health centre.

'What's wrong with a boat with a hole in it?' I replied. He tutted and went back to the sports pages.

'What's wrong with me studying?' I asked. 'It was your idea in the first place.'

'You didn't enjoy it,' he said. 'It made you tired and grumpy.'

'I did enjoy it,' I said. 'I loved it.'

'Only when you'd passed. When you were doing it you were tired and grumpy.'

'*You* get tired and grumpy,' I said.

'Not from choice,' he replied. I held fire to consider my position. I could see the crisis looming. It was the crisis that had loomed briefly on our wedding night when he had asked me to give up my stage career and it had only been avoided then because I didn't have one. I recalled his opposition to me taking the job I had, which he had reconciled himself to because it was only dabbling. George, I decided, didn't want me to have a life of my own. He didn't believe in my advancement or my independence. He wanted me At Home, poor.

While I was reaching this conclusion Diana from the maths class asked me if I wanted to go on a weekend creative writing course. She said it would be good for me, especially if I was going to do my English O-levels. I said to George, 'It will be a big help with my English O-levels.'

He said, 'Be realistic, Tessa. I'm very proud of you but you have two small children. You've proved you can do it. If you must do something else do art. You like art.'

'I'm not going to do art,' I said. 'I'm going to do English. And I'm going on the course. You've got your O-levels. Let me get mine.'

'I got my O-levels,' he snapped, 'when I didn't have any obligations towards a family.' Then he stopped talking.

The issue went into cold storage for a few days and wasn't referred to. This is how George likes things that are dangerous and years of experience have taught me that forcing a confrontation only makes him retreat further. He is a man who likes to deal with things in his own time or not at all, which is infinitely preferable.

Eventually he said, 'When did you say your course was?' I breathed a sigh of relief and told him, not so much because I wanted to go as because I wanted him to let me. He smiled with delight.

'What a shame,' he said. 'That's the weekend of my concert.'

'What concert?' I asked in disbelief.

'Mick's concert,' he said. Mick is his trumpet teacher. 'I'm playing "Danny Boy". I was going to surprise you.'

'I'm surprised,' I said.

'You'll come, won't you?' he said. 'You wouldn't miss it. I couldn't do it without you.'

'That's blackmail,' I said.

'It's a bloody concert,' he shouted. And he stopped talking again. This silence was a big silence, a silence as deep and as heavy as the Pope's thoughts on Zen.

I put up with it as long as I could, which was until Diana rang to say she had to book for the course and could I come. I said I would let her know when George

179

came home. 'We have to talk about it,' I said to him over supper.

'What is there to say?' he said. 'You know what this concert means to me.'

'About the same as my course means to me,' I suggested.

'Don't be silly,' he sniffed. 'There's no comparison.'

'There is a comparison,' I argued. 'What you want to do compared to what I want to do.'

'You have always resented my trumpet,' he said. 'You think you are the artistic one.'

'What?' I said. 'You know that's ridiculous. I've never tried to stop you playing it. You are trying to stop me doing O-levels.'

'I'm not stopping you,' he said. 'I'm just pointing out that when you study you're a pain to live with.'

'Time is slipping by,' I said. 'There's more to life than just working, eating and sleeping.'

'O-levels are working,' he said. 'My music is a major achievement.' He sighed. 'I really want you to be there, Tessa. Please come.'

Someone had to give in so I did. It's not every day you get to hear your husband playing 'Danny Boy' on the trumpet in public for the first time. He was very nervous and could barely walk to the centre of Mick's living-room. Katy called out, 'There's my Daddy,' which couldn't have helped. But he did it and we all clapped like mad. So did the twelve other members of the audience who were related to the three other performers.

There will be other courses in creative writing though I can't say I'm wildly drawn to them. It wasn't so much the course as the principle that was at stake, George's acceptance of the future of my brain. When the concert was over and we were toasting his success he said, 'It was worth hanging round for, wasn't it?' I said it was. He said, 'Now you're going to do more O-levels.' I said I was. He said, 'I suppose we'll get used to it,' and added, 'You wouldn't consider the trombone, would you?'

I might one day when the personal growing stops and we go back to hand-in-hand, if we ever go back to it. I don't think it's something you can go back to. I think you move on to arm-in-arm. Arm-in-arm is how you move through a marriage when you are grown up.

CHAPTER NINETEEN

Viyella Woman

We took a second honeymoon to celebrate our tenth wedding anniversary. We couldn't afford Spain so we went to the Lake District for a week. It was George's idea. 'Ten years is a long time,' he explained.

His parents moved in to look after the children, the rabbits and the fish. Hatty said sadly, 'Ten years. It has aged him.' She will never get over it.

I said, 'Will the Escort make it up the motorway? Why haven't we got a new car?'

George said, 'I hope you have sheets without holes in them for Mum and Dad.'

Honeymoons aren't the same after ten years of marriage. The tension is different. The mystery has gone. There are so many other people to consider. The children wanted to know why they couldn't come.

'We need you to look after the animals,' George told them. 'You'll be with Granma and Granpa. You'll like that.'

'Granma and Granpa could look after the animals,' Christopher said. 'You could pay them.'

George said, 'Look! Mummy and I are going away for a rest. You want us to have a rest, don't you?'

'I'm tired too,' Christopher said.

George said when we were alone that he didn't really

want a rest. He wanted a honeymoon like the last one. His capacity for fond memories defies belief. He fondly remembers chicken-pox. I didn't remind him that our last honeymoon was as restful as a cruise in a typhoon because I wanted a holiday. I told myself that this one would be different because we were older and wiser.

I stopped feeling older and wiser the minute we hit the motorway and I was assailed by the sort of guilt I remembered from smoking in the loo when I was fourteen. A second honeymoon began to feel like something I definitely shouldn't be doing. 'Do you feel wicked?' I said to George, coyly putting my hand on his thigh. 'George?'

He said, 'Can you hear a tapping noise in the engine?' I removed my hand. I said I couldn't hear anything. He said I must be able to. It was going, 'Tap, tap, tap.' I said I couldn't. He said I must be deaf and he drove for thirty miles with his ear to the dashboard, willing me to hear it and swerving on to the hard shoulder so cars in the slow lane could speed by. Eventually he said he didn't like it and we pulled off the motorway at the next exit to find a garage. The man said it would take four hours to fix.

'It's no use complaining,' George said. 'It could be a lot worse. They might have had to take it in for days.'

'I'm not complaining,' I said.

'Your face is complaining,' he pointed out. After ten years of marriage there is no disguising faces.

Four hours later we headed back on to the motorway for the long haul north. We didn't say much. I stared out the window and marvelled at the hands Life deals. Ten years ago I would have sworn that at thirty I would be a household name. But there I was, a household fixture, bolted into place for the rest of my life. Even more amazing, I was hardly protesting at all.

I marvelled at George still being my husband, despite being the man he is. Not much about him had changed.

He was a bit fatter and tattier. He was still at Mathesons, even if he was now quite important, which he hadn't been for over nine years. He was still a man who liked to eat and sleep, even if he now played the trumpet.

I compared my life to Jennifer's. Ten years ago she was a girl on the way up with a mind of her own and her future assured. Then she became a wife and mother extraordinaire, then an injured wife and struggling mother, then a wife with a career, then a faithless wife and now she is separated with children to raise and a job to do. George and I had our ups and downs but they were tiny compared to hers. For all the excitement in her life I wouldn't trade places with her. After ten years I liked being a woman with a family and a husband.

'It's back again,' George said after a couple more hours. 'Can you hear it?'

'No,' I said. 'Why didn't we hire a car? I said this one wouldn't make it.'

'It's been perfectly reliable for three years,' he said.

'Then force it to get us to the Lakes,' I snarled. After ten years of marriage there is no real excuse for manners. Familiarity breeds an awful lot to put up with.

An hour later we drove off the motorway for the second time so George could raise the bonnet with the air of a man who knows what he is going to find beneath it. 'It's only a noise,' I cried. 'Why can't we keep driving with a noise I can't even hear?'

'Because it is dangerous,' George said.

'Why don't we just get our bags and leave it here?' I called out the window. He ignored me. 'George,' I yelled. 'I am cold and tired and hungry. This is horrible.'

'Shut up,' he said. He had nothing to lose. It was a second honeymoon after all. He wandered along the road looking for a phone box to call the AA man, who arrived an hour later and found the trouble immediately. It was a toy spanner of Christopher's rattling around in the engine. George seemed to flirt with the idea of dying of humiliation but he pulled himself together and thanked the man for his trouble. When he had gone he said, 'Only you would allow a child to play with a car engine.' We reached the small hotel without speaking another word.

It was a very nice hotel and very pretty but dinner was long over by the time we arrived. The receptionist said there might be something open in the town. 'I'm not hungry,' I said.

'Well I am,' George snapped. We sat on our twin beds and glared at each other.

'After ten years,' I said, 'we are back where we started.' George laughed.

'At least we're here,' he said. 'Come on, let's go and eat.'

We strolled through the town looking for somewhere romantic and candle-lit to begin celebrating our ten years but everything was shut. We settled for a pizza, which we ate on a park bench in the biting wind and we groped for significant things to say.

'Did you leave enough rabbit food?' George asked.

'I suppose so,' I said. 'Did you tell them about the garbage?'

What did we talk about on our first honeymoon when there were no rabbits and no garbage? It must have been on George's mind as well. Before we went to sleep he said, 'This is the tenth anniversary of the night before our wedding.'

'That is very clever of you,' I said. I was relieved we had stopped sulking. I wanted a carefree week and I was looking forward to giving George his present.

I had saved for it. It was a camera to replace the cheap camera that had replaced the one that had been stolen so many years before. It wasn't the very best money could buy because I didn't have that much money, but it was the best I could afford and I was pleased with it. I hoped George had bought me something I could keep.

We ordered breakfast in bed and it was over breakfast that George produced his neatly wrapped package, which was soft and squidgy and about a foot square, just like all the other presents he had ever bought me. 'Not another night dress,' I said to myself, hardly believing that it would be. But it was. A viyella nightie with pink and yellow flowers that buttoned to the neck. I wanted to weep. All the other nighties have been flimsy and see-through, sexy nighties from a husband to his wife. This nightie was fit for a nun. After ten years I had become a woman George preferred to see in viyella. I had become Viyella Woman. 'It looks very warm,' I said.

He opened his present and I began to smile with anticipation at the pleasure it would give him. 'I know what it is,' he grinned as the wrapping fell away, but his grin fell away with the wrapping.

'Oh,' he said. 'Very nice.'

'Is it what you were expecting?' I asked, less chuffed than I had hoped to be.

'A camera,' he said flatly, 'Yes, thanks very much. I thought it would be a camera.' He turned it over in his hands as if it was a diamond that had shrunk on contact with his flesh. 'It just isn't the one I thought.'

'We can always change it,' I said.

'I wouldn't dream of it,' he said, summoning a faint smile. 'The one I was thinking of costs far too much.'

We sat there in the wrapping paper and gave consideration to the gifts that represented our love after ten years. I stroked the awful nightie which I might have given my mother and he studied the camera which wasn't the one he had longed for.

'You don't really like the nightie, do you?' he said.

'You can't dislike a nightie.' I said, 'But I've never actually needed one that kept me warm. You're not planning on single beds, are you?'

'Of course not,' he said, staring at the camera. This wasn't a pretty sight: two middle-aged people among the marmalade sulking over their presents like a couple of ungrateful children. Even then I could see how pathetic it was. You don't grieve over ill-considered presents when you are thirty. But we did.

I did especially, because not only had George given me yet another nightie, he had given me one that insulted the image I thought he had of me after ten years. And not only didn't he care much for the camera, it didn't seem to occur to him that I had scrimped for it in a way that he certainly hadn't had to scrimp for the hideous viyella.

The presents, I said to myself as I wept in the bathroom, were like our marriage. We had unwrapped the contents of the packages we had taken until death did us part and we had found them lacking. What I had given George was only a cheaper version of what he had actually wanted. What he had given me was dull, prematurely ageing and wrong. This is where we stand, I told myself, after ten years, and we must make the most of it. I suppose I was still tired.

After breakfast we went for a long, bracing walk on which George got a blister and had to be half-carried home. We didn't say a lot to each other except, 'Look at the view' and 'I wonder how the children are.' We tried to pretend that the presents hadn't been exchanged and that we were a normal, happy couple spending a few days together in the Lakes. Because we weren't speaking we had plenty of time to think. I suppose George was thinking. He might have been chewing his cud. It is the same expression.

I went back to examining the ten years we were celebrating, beginning with our first honeymoon and my terrible tantrums, the fainting, my disappointment, his disappointment and the passion that had drawn us together in the first place. I thought about our first home together and how I had hated it and our second home and how much I had loved it.

I thought about the furniture we had bought together, the hours we had put in together deciding how to run our lives and function for the best. I thought about the compromises we had both had to make and how he had come to tolerate my excesses and listen to my turmoil and how I had grown used to his silences and to appreciate his strength, which appeared unexpectedly when I most needed it.

I thought about the children and how the people who had had them were George and me, the very people who had been on honeymoon together in Spain and who were this very minute sitting opposite each other in silence over a bottle of house white, fish and a small unlit candle.

I thought about Paul Nolan and Mrs Ferguson's brother, who seemed insignificant among the mountains and the lakes, and I thought about Mrs Sparrow's house and how George was living there when he would much rather have done the sensible thing and run a mile from it.

I thought about his trumpet, my studying and where our personal growth was taking us and I realized that even if I was moving on in my own erratic way, it was nice to know that he was there, moving on in his way, which wasn't ever erratic. I tried to imagine the future but couldn't without him because he was so much a part of my past and present.

I looked at his face, which really wasn't very much older but which was very familiar. He put his hand on mine and smiled. 'What are you thinking about?' he said.

'The past,' I said. 'And the future.'

'What about the past and the future?' he asked.

'I was thinking that the past was sweet and the future rosy,' I said. He lifted his glass.

'Here's to the honey,' he said.

'And the moon,' I replied.

All Futura Books are available at your bookshop or newsagent, or can be ordered from the following address: Futura Books, Cash Sales Department, P.O. Box 11, Falmouth, Cornwall.

Please send cheque or postal order (no currency), and allow 55p for postage and packing for the first book plus 22p for the second book and 14p for each additional book ordered up to a maximum charge of £1.75 in U.K.

Customers in Eire and B.F.P.O. please allow 55p for the first book, 22p for the second book plus 14p per copy for the next 7 books, thereafter 8p per book.

Overseas customers please allow £1 for postage and packing for the first book and 25p per copy for each additional book.